HUNTING THE HEADHUNTERS

A WOMAN'S GUIDE

DIANE COLE

A Fireside Book
Published by Simon & Schuster Inc.
New York   London   Toronto   Sydney   Tokyo

Fireside
Simon & Schuster Building
Rockefeller Center
1230 Avenue of the Americas
New York, New York 10020

Published by the Simon & Schuster Trade Division

FIRESIDE and colophon are registered trademarks
of Simon & Schuster Inc.

Designed by Kathy Kikkert

Manufactured in the United States of America

10   9   8   7   6   5   4   3   2   1

Library of Congress Cataloging in Publication Data

Cole, Diane.
    Hunting the headhunters : a woman's guide / Diane Cole.
        p.   cm.
    "A Fireside book."
    ISBN 0-671-64238-3
    1. Recruiting of employees.   2. Women executives—Recruiting.
3. Career development.   I. Title.
HF5549.5.R44C56   1988
650.1'4'024042—dc19   88-15764
                                                            CIP

ISBN 0-671-64238-3

For Dad, for Peter,
and in memory of my mother,
Roselda Katz Cole

ACKNOWLEDGMENTS

Every book is a journey. There are a number of people without whom this particular book would not have been possible, and many others without whom this journey would not have proved half so interesting or enjoyable.

I would like to thank everyone who generously and graciously gave their time and help: all of the executive recruiters, researchers, professional career counselors, and many women and men who shared their job-hunting experiences with me.

Special thanks are due to Jeanne Marie Gilbert, Marge Baxter, Dee Soder, and Kenneth Cole. Thank you once again to Wendy Reid Crisp, Thomas Ogdon, Ann Powers Kern, Martha Green, Howard Williams, Kathleen Lusk Brooke, Carol Kanarek, Gracemarie Soper, Sydney Reynolds, Camille Lavington, Jean Boler, Howard Stevens, Allan D. R. Stern, Chris Stevens, Nella Barkley, Alice Early, Janet Jones-Parker, and James Kennedy. Another thank you, too, to those who preferred to remain anonymous and the many others who found time to answer my questions.

Further thanks to my agent, Susan Lee Cohen; to David Vigliano; and to my editor, Barbara Gess.

And a very special continuing thank you to all the family members, friends, and writing and business buddies who gave support and encouragement throughout this project.

Most of all, thanks to my husband—for being there and for everything else.

CONTENTS

CHAPTER 4: CULTIVATING THE HEADHUNTERS: HOW TO HELP THEM SO THAT THEY CAN HELP YOU 109

CHAPTER 5: WHEN THE CALL COMES: THE ETIQUETTE OF THE CHASE 130

CHAPTER 6: CAREFUL OR YOU MIGHT GET SCALPED: WARNINGS AND CAVEATS AND SOME FINAL WORDS

CHAPTER 7: YOUR DATA BANK: LISTINGS AND RESOURCES

INTRODUCTION

FIRST THINGS FIRST: WHY THIS BOOK?

"So you're writing a book about headhunters! I'd really appreciate it if you could tell me which ones to call!"

"What do you mean, the title of your book is *Hunting the Headhunters*? Don't you have to wait for them to call you?"

"God, I'd love to know how to get plugged in! I hate looking for jobs."

"Oh, headhunters! I sure could tell you some stories—if you'd want to print them!"

"Headhunters? What's a headhunter?"

"Sure, I could tell you about headhunters—that's how I found the job I'm in now."

As I worked on *Hunting the Headhunters*, these were the refrains, repeated again and again. I heard them at professional meetings, cocktail parties, social gatherings—anywhere I happened to mention the topic of my book. For every positive story about a job placement through an executive recruiter, I received at least twice as many queries for names and numbers of whom to call, and heard about as many complaints about experiences with headhunters. These patterns became so pronounced that after a while, I began to believe that the hunger for knowledge about the industry was only equaled by the number of misconceptions about it. Very quickly I discovered that headhunters were either idealized as job-bestowing gods and goddesses or villainized as the executive suite equivalent

15

of used-car salesmen plying jobs instead of jalopies.

As in most cases, the truth lies somewhere in between. There were more than enough stories to gratify the boosters, yet I also came across tales that seemed designed to satisfy the detractors. There was plenty to convince me of the industry's merits and to demonstrate the benefits that a headhunter's friendship can yield. Yet I also heard a sufficient number of caveats and warnings—even from those within the industry—to encourage in me a healthy dose of skepticism.

Why does even the mention of the executive-recruiting industry so often stir such mixed, and often negative, responses? In the same way that some folks lump all lawyers together as a bad lot, executive recruiters are often tossed together (and frequently by executives who should know better) in a rotten barrel labeled *Headhunters*.

Why such a lack of information and understanding among otherwise well-informed executives? Perhaps it's due to the fact that the executive-search industry is relatively new, and therefore may still be considered something of a phenomenon. The oldest firm, Thorndike Deland Associates, may have originated in the 1920s, but the largest in the world, Korn/Ferry International, was established only in 1969.

Perhaps it's not surprising, then, that when Lester B. Korn, cofounder and chairman of Korn/Ferry, was appointed to be the U.S. representative to the Economic and Social Council of the United Nations in July 1987, the *Wall Street Journal* reported that, "Competitors say they welcome the increasing respectability that Mr. Korn's ascension to the rank of ambassador could bring to the headhunting business," a business, the story commented, "once viewed as slightly disreputable."[1]

The rapid growth and expansion of the whole recruiting industry may also help account for the fact that its rules of etiquette as well as its ethical standards are often debated. Is persuading an executive to leave one company and join a competitor really recruiting—or is it corporate "raiding"? Or is the

---

[1] *The Wall Street Journal*, July 16, 1987.

executive recruiter merely the handy scapegoat for the embarrassed loser in this corporate game?

There are other questions, as well. Are recruiters paid, in part, to ask the illegal interview questions that the companies themselves don't want to ask? How do the recruiters and their research departments manage to get their hands on so much information about so many executives, anyway? Finally, once you've established contact with the recruiter, should you worry that your resume will be distributed without your knowledge and consent?

"There are some bad actors that exist and will continue to, you can't stop them—we're an unregulated industry," says John H. Dugan, the chairman of the National Association of Executive Recruiters, "but the majority maintain a good ethical standard, and I believe that [attitude]'s increasing." To help maintain those standards, professional associations like the NAER, the Association of Executive Search Consultants, and the National Association of Corporate and Professional Recruiters all advance guidelines for professional and ethical behavior.

These guidelines exist because the executive-recruiting industry has become a corporate fact of life, a growing industry that is apparently here to stay. Its exact size, however, is difficult to determine.

One leading authority, James H. Kennedy, editor and publisher of the widely read industry newsletter, *Executive Recruiter News*, says there are about two thousand firms in existence and that the industry as a whole is about a two-billion-dollar a year business. Another expert, Kenneth J. Cole, publisher of *Recruiting and Search Report*, estimates the industry to be a four-billion-dollar a year business, with the number of firms approaching nine thousand. And Paul Hawkinson, publisher of the *Fordyce Letter*, a newsletter addressed to personnel professionals, says that the total number of all types of third-party agencies—"from Bob's Jobs to Korn/Ferry," as he puts it—may be closer to 26,000 firms.

Whatever statistics you use, however, the message remains

the same. Thousands of client companies hire executive recruiters to fill thousands of jobs—positions you will not see
advertised in the daily classifieds or hear about from employment agencies.

Recruiters fill many positions, but they do not work with
even a majority of all job openings. James Kennedy, for instance, estimates that the industry as a whole handles approximately eighty to a hundred thousand positions a year, or about
10 to 15 percent of all job vacancies. That is only a small
chunk of the total market, but considering the level of many of
the searches that firms conduct, it is also one that cannot be
ignored. For if you do ignore the recruiters' calls, you are also
ignoring a small but significant chunk of job opportunities that
might be available to you.

For this reason, the search business is an industry which
executives who wish to be aware of all job market possibilities
would do well to learn to turn to their own advantage.

But how do you gain the attention of an executive recruiter?
How do you get the headhunter to hunt you? *Hunting the
Headhunters* presents one strategy for women who wish to
take the next step in their careers.

And now you ask: *Why women?*

Certainly much of the information contained in this book
can be equally applied to men and to women. That is how it
should be.

Further, regardless of sex, whether or not you are currently
looking to change jobs, there is a good chance that you will be
looking in the near future. Job changing has been a growing
trend for the last decade. According to a 1978 study by the
College Board, 53 percent of all adults between the ages of 25
and 39 were planning to change either their jobs or their careers. Statistics from the U. S. Department of Labor, Bureau of
Labor Statistics show that in 1983, the median stay with any
given employer was less than five years. And by 1987, a recruiter at Spencer Stuart, one of the country's largest recruiting
firms, was telling the *Wall Street Journal* that in the future
managers will hold seven to ten jobs over the course of their

careers. As recently as the 1970s, that figure would have been three or four.[2]

There is also a growing trend for companies to seek executives who have worked in more than one company, as either a way to mark the breadth of their experience or a sign of their ability to work in different corporate cultures. Lester B. Korn noted this trend in a speech delivered to the Wharton and Columbia Business School Clubs in 1985, and a number of recruiters spoke of it in interviews for this book.

Of course, not all job changes are voluntary. Corporate takeovers and mergers and acquisitions have been the stuff of headlines for several years now. An entire industry—the outplacement business—has grown precisely in response to the large number of executives squeezed out of corporations that want to become, in the phrase of the day, "leaner and meaner." Many thousands of executives have been laid off from companies which quickly discover after a merger takes place that they need only one rather than two corporate counsels or heads of research, or one instead of two departments of public relations, strategic planning, information systems, and so on.

The ax can fall anywhere, but it is staff positions rather than line roles with fiscal responsibility that tend to go first. And these are the very positions to which many women traditionally have gravitated.

Regardless of your job title, however, the extraordinary number of mergers and acquisitions in recent years should make every executive aware of the precariousness of even the most seemingly secure position. For this reason, when a corporate takeover or company-wide reorganization looms, a friendly headhunter may be one friend you will be glad to have.

In the chapters that follow, you will learn how to use the headhunter in your specific job hunt. You will discover what recruiters are looking for and what you should look for in a recruiter. You will learn how to become visible to recruiters,

---

[2]*The Wall Street Journal*, May 19, 1987.

prepare for the interview, present yourself to your best advantage, and develop and maintain ongoing business relationships with recruiters who may not have a position suitable for you now, but may in the future.

You will also be advised to be selective. Although companies may be looking for executives who have worked in more than one company, a stigma is still attached to people who have switched jobs excessively. Not every job offer—and not every recruiter—will be right for you. And since there are some "bad players," you must be on guard against possible breaches of confidentiality that might jeopardize your current position.

It is also important to keep the recruiter's role, what recruiters can do for you and what they cannot, in perspective. First, although executive recruiters can be an important resource for the executive seeking to change jobs, since they do handle only a small percentage of all job openings, a "headhunter strategy" is only one of many to consider in planning your career as a whole.

Further, headhunters should not be confused with career counselors; they are not in the business of giving advice but of filling jobs for their client companies. As a job seeker, you are best advised to discover what you're looking for *before* you speak to a headhunter. To this end, the first chapter will provide you with a broader context for planning what comes next.

Whether you are male or female, all of this advice will apply equally.

In spite of the great strides women have made in the last decade, however, prejudice and discrimination remain a force in the workplace. For instance, even though more fields than ever are open to women, the highest concentration of women in a given company will often still be found in staff roles, and as previously mentioned these jobs are usually also the first to be cut in the wake of the "reorganization" following a merger or takeover. Rather than waiting to receive a pink slip, however, the executive who has already built a relationship with a

headhunter may find herself one step ahead of other colleagues scrambling for new jobs.

Another "special issue" for women has to do with family
and child-care responsibilities. How do you address the un-
asked questions in many prospective employers' minds: *Will
she leave to have children and raise her family? If she has
children already, how dependable will she be? Just how com-
mitted is she?*

Of course, questions regarding child care and family responsibility apply to men as well as women. But fair or not, legal or
not, these are still the questions that women, more often than
men, must be prepared to answer.

Beyond these issues, are there any differences between the
ways men and women deal with recruiters? A number of recruiters comment that more women than men tend to have
difficulty with the initial phone call or interview. They point
to differences in presentation and self-confidence, in knowing
how to make themselves visible, and in understanding how to
play the headhunter game in general.

One can see how some recruiters could quite naturally and
innocently come to this conclusion. Say a recruiter, trying to
identify potential job candidates in an industry in which men
outnumber women, calls two women and five men. One
woman refuses to answer the call, as does one man. And there
you have it: 50 percent of the women have been unhelpful, as
compared to only 20 percent of the men.

Further, since many women still have only recently begun
reaching high levels of job responsibility, there are also increasingly more women who are receiving phone calls from
headhunters for the first time, learning the rules of yet another
new sport, making mistakes as every new player must. This
book will guide that first-time player, male or female.

Do recruiters perceive still other differences between men
and women? Interestingly, one high-level recruiter identifies
what she calls the woman's "nesting instinct." "Once they're
comfortable at a job, they're much harder to convince to move

than men," she says. And, she implies, they also are less likely to aggressively pursue the next step in their careers.

Other recruiters and career counselors comment that although it is the easiest thing in the world for *anyone* to become comfortable and complacent, to become so immersed in the present that no thought is given to the future, they believe that women tend to bury their heads in their in-boxes more than men. Further, they say, women are less successful in taking the long view of their careers; and in spite of all the articles written about women and networking, many women still believe that developing mutually beneficial business relationships—including ones with headhunters—borders on using people.

Are these observations verifiable as facts, or are they merely commonly held opinions? Perceptions, whether true or false, unfortunately can sometimes count more than facts. And all too often women must still fight to counter more misperceptions than men.

In researching *Hunting the Headhunters*, I interviewed executive recruiters as well as executives who have been approached and recruited by them. I also spoke to executives who have hired recruiters, to career counselors, and to various industry experts. By showing you the headhunting business from these different angles, I hope not only to present you with one strategy for career advancement, but also to encourage you to explore and pursue the many career resources available to you, and, ultimately, to place these career goals within the broader context of how you wish to live your life as a whole. With this in mind, we begin.

HUNTING THE HEADHUNTERS

1
WHY A HEADHUNTER?

BEFORE THE SAFARI BEGINS...

Headhunter: The word conjures images of cutthroat cannibals and savage rites, of bloody scalps and neatly preserved skulls —a subject that sounds chillingly perfect for a late-night flick, but not even remotely related to the idea of career advancement.

Yet the mid-career executive might do well to dream of a special breed of headhunter: executive recruiters who stalk their prey in the jungles of corporate and professional America.

The best metaphor for these highly paid individuals may be that of matchmaker. In essence, they are professional go-betweens, job brokers hired and paid by client companies to fill vacancies for high- and mid-level executive positions that most people are not likely to read about in the classifieds or hear about through the grapevine.

Partly because of the profession's nicknames, partly because it is more common for a search consultant to seek rather than to be sought by a job prospect (or, in the parlance of the trade, a candidate), a mystique has arisen about the executive-search industry. The mystery lies in who is chosen to be called and how. Supposedly, one must wait passively, shuffling memos and twiddling one's thumbs while opportunity knocks on someone else's office door.

Like most mystiques, though, this one is fueled as much by mythology as reality. Although many executive recruiters cringe at the term headhunter—it's hardly a compliment to be thought of as a member of a bloodthirsty tribe—they are, in a very real sense, hungry. They are hungry for talented people to fill their clients' vacant executive chairs. To satisfy this need, they feed on the names of qualified professionals. They need sales managers and lawyers, marketing directors and advertising VPs, computer specialists and hospital directors, public-relations executives and financial managers. They hunt, track, and pursue qualified professionals to fill managerial chairs in the offices of companies in all fifty states.

They might be hunting you.

You need not play the passive quarry, however. After all, you need not—and should not—play a passive role in your career or in your life as a whole.

And you need not wait with idle expectation for a recruiter to discover you. There are a number of ways to bring yourself to their attention and encourage them to seek you. And then, once you have sparked their interest, you need not jump at every offer made to you. The point is to take an active role in the game of executive headhunting—and at the same time take an active role in planning your career.

WHAT RECRUITERS CAN DO FOR YOU: SOME HAPPY ENDINGS

1.

"Hello, my name is Rich Opportunity from Search-the-World, Incorporated. We've been retained by a client company to fill a position in your area and I wondered if you'd be interested in talking for a few minutes?"

Whenever she received such calls, Linda S.[1], a skeptic by

---

[1] The names and identifying details of some of these executives have been changed.

nature, tended to think that she did not want to talk. Having gained an expertise in product development while working at a large Boston-based consulting firm, Linda, in her early thirties, possessed an unusual combination of technical knowledge and experience that attracted several such calls a year.

Although Linda did not recognize the caller's name, she knew his firm to have a good reputation among her colleagues. "I'm happy where I am," she said, "but I'm willing to listen."

At an informal meeting the next day, the caller told her that he had been retained by a local investment advisory firm looking for someone to head its marketing department. "Quite frankly, they're starting the whole department from scratch, and at the moment they're not exactly sure who they're looking for. But the particular position they've asked me to fill for them—to head that department—is, I think, at a more senior level than would be right for you at this moment.

"But they are looking for good people, and they will need to staff the rest of that new department," he continued. "At this point, I realize, it might be more helpful to *them* than to you to talk to them—to give them ideas for what that department might be like. But would you be willing to come in just to meet the people and see what happens?"

Although she doubted anything *would* happen, Linda agreed. First of all, the newly formed company had a reputation for innovation. Second, what did she have to lose by simply meeting people from the company? Finally, the request had been posed as a favor—and why not be in the good graces of a recruiter from a prestigious firm?

"The first interview lasted about two and a half hours and a lot of it was just what the recruiter had said it would be: their picking my brain about the projects they were planning and their feasibility," Linda recalls. "But in focusing on *their* problems, I ended up talking a lot about what *I* do, too. After we had talked for a while, the company president called in other people to meet me as well."

Still, no job was offered, and Linda forgot about it. "It was clear they needed someone more senior than I to head the department, and so even though I had a good feeling about the company, I adopted this attitude that nothing would probably come of it." Had she wasted her time?

Two months later the recruiter called again. "They're finally about to make an offer to someone to head that department, and they'd like you to talk to that person when he accepts. Would you be interested in talking about being the department's second in command?"

Linda calculated that as second in command of a new department in a growing company, she would possess far greater responsibility than she would for some years to come in her current company with its highly structured corporate hierarchy. She had been impressed by the executives she had met at the new firm; clearly that impression had been mutual. Moreover, the position would be a challenge, and part of the challenge would be in defining and developing this new aspect of the company's business.

Yes, she said, she would be interested in talking further.

"I would not have heard of or be in this position except for the recruiter," she acknowledges. She has worked for the new company for the last two years.

2.

After several years at a fast-growing high-tech company, Sally K. realized she had risen about as far as she could go. It wasn't that there was no room for her within the company itself—there was plenty she wanted to do, and she had ideas all the time. The problem was that she had been tagged as Sally K., head of publications, and her proposals to get involved with the marketing or other aspects of the company fell on deaf ears. With great sadness, she decided it was time to find another job.

Through her friends, she got the names of two recruiters with whom they had worked, and before long she heard from both of them. The first sent her on an interview to a company similar to her own. "The feedback was good," she recalls. "The executives were impressed, the headhunter told me, but they wanted someone more 'status quo,' by which he meant someone who would keep things the way they always had been in that department. That was helpful—it was our philosophies that didn't match, not my ability. But I never heard from that recruiter again."

Meanwhile, through the second recruiter, Sally had met with the executives of another high-tech company. This time, the philosophies were the same—but the position was not at a level high enough to induce Sally to make a switch.

And that, she thought, was the end of both leads.

"Then, about three months later, I got a call back from that second company. They had remembered me. Another, higher-level position had come up. Would I be interested in talking to them again? Of course. And since the recruiter was the one who had introduced me to the company to begin with, he entered the picture again, too."

After another series of interviews, an offer was made. It would mean about a 20-percent increase in compensation, and more important, a better career opportunity. Not only would she head a larger department than she had run before, but because of the way the job was structured, she would also carry greater clout. In addition, she would have the opportunity to become involved with the development of a new product. It was a position, in short, designed to help her move up in the company and be a part of its management team—not just stay in place.

3.

Jane H. had toiled for seven years in the Connecticut office of a large New York law firm when she received the phone call that led to her current position as general counsel for a major utility company.

"I was very lucky," she says. But was it only luck?

When she received the recruiter's call she had been actively looking for a new job for several months. She had gone on several interviews. She had seen at least one recruiter, an interview which she thought was "a total waste of time." She had even had a job offer that she had refused because it wasn't right.

"Well, so if it wasn't luck, it was pure networking," she says, amending her first statement after another moment's thought. You see, in addition to pursuing all her other job leads, Jane had put out the word to a selective group of friends and colleagues that she wanted to switch jobs. And not only that, she had told these friends *exactly* what she was looking for, so that they would know what to listen for on her behalf and when to mention her name.

So when the recruiter called Jane's friend as a source for a corporate counsel position for a large company in Connecticut, her friend knew just whose name to mention.

"I'd say I get calls from three or four recruiters every few months," Jane says now, "not to see if I want a new job, but to see if I can help them come up with some names. You know—they're networking. That's how that recruiter found me three years ago, and you bet I help them with names. Because if, at some point in the future, I want to look again, *I'll* be able to call them."

4.

"I'm extremely happy at my job and not the least bit interested in changing," Wendy Reid Crisp, then editor of *Savvy Magazine*, told the recruiter for at least the second time.

The more enthusiastically Crisp spoke, the more interested the recruiter became. "At least let's have lunch and let me describe this to you!" the recruiter insisted. "How much time would that take?"

At their meeting the next day, the recruiter pitched the job— directing a publishing product development and marketing program—and described the potential salary structure and compensation package. One drawback loomed larger than any of the benefits, however: the job required moving from the New York area. Crisp said no.

"But a very interesting thing happened," Crisp relates. "I had been told what a valuable person I was, both in terms of job responsibility and money. They wanted me to do marketing and PR, to develop products and design strategies—the very things I wanted to do but had no opportunity to do where I was.

"And that got me thinking. If this company wants me to do that for them, why can't I do that for myself? It made a tremendous difference in how I assessed my career."

The company's interest in her helped Crisp crystallize her thoughts about the future and acted as a catalyst. It also tested her in the job market and showed her how the publishing community at large viewed her abilities. "It changed everything," she says simply. "It's the reason I'm sitting where I am now."

For within two months of that phone call, Crisp had resigned from her position at *Savvy* and announced the formation of her own publishing company, New Chapter Press.

"So there are a lot of things you can get from a headhunter besides a job," Crisp laughs.

One of them is a way to define your career anew.

5.

After a year of a not entirely romantic commute between her job in New York City and her fiancé, who lived in a large Midwestern city, Susan S., a high-ranking executive at a non-profit organization, decided to tie the knot and move permanently to the Midwest.

"Call my friend—he's a headhunter who works with nonprofits," a colleague at another organization told her. "We've used him a few times, and he might be able to help you."

He did help, but not in the way that Susan had expected.

"I'm not handling anything in that part of the country that might suit you right now," he told his disappointed listener. "But here are the names of a few people you might call when you get there. They might know of something—" And he proceeded to open his Rolodex and reel off several names to her.

Was it a favor? Yes—not to Susan, however, but to the mutual friend who had referred her. What was in it for the recruiter? Well, some good will from a client who will remember him all the better the next time she has a position to fill.

And, of course, when Susan finds herself in a position to retain a recruiter, chances are she'll remember him, too.

WHAT RECRUITERS CANNOT DO FOR YOU: SOME MISTAKEN BEGINNINGS

If the previous stories demonstrate the opportunities and possibilities that executive recruiters can present, the following scenarios dramatize the mistaken assumptions that many people have about the services that they can and cannot provide.

1.

After graduating from law school and spending several years as an associate in one of her city's largest firms, Carol M. made a startling discovery about herself: The practice of law bored her. She wasn't exactly sure what she wanted, only that she wanted out of the firm, perhaps out of law altogether.

Where to go now, she wondered? A colleague gave her the name of a recruiter who specialized in the legal field and suggested that she call.

When she explained that she was looking for guidance, however, the recruiter was polite but firm. "We're executive recruiters, not career counselors," the headhunter explained to her. "Our clients are looking for people who love what they're doing and have a track record besides. When you've figured out what you want from your career and are on your way to achieving those goals," he continued, "that's when a recruiter can begin to help you."

2.

As a data-processing manager, Alice J. was used to receiving several calls a year from headhunters. The industry was hot and she was hot. Why even bother returning the calls? She didn't need them; they needed her.

This was true until the day the new department head walked into her office and explained that the project she had worked on so diligently for the last nine months was now completed, and so was the company's need for her services. He hated to do it, but times were tough and he would have to lay her off.

Well, that was all right, she thought, remembering all the pink message slips from recruiters she had thrown away in the last year.

But when she called one of the headhunters who had called her before, the response was not quite what she had hoped. "Of course, we'd be interested in talking to someone with your background and experience," the recruiter told her. "But you realize that things are tight all over right now. I'm not working on a suitable search right now, and of course, even in the best of times, no recruiter can promise to find a position for someone immediately! But come in and talk, and I'll certainly keep you in mind."

3.

After spending several years as the editorial director of a Fortune 500 company, Stephanie B. had come to feel that her staff position was somewhat limited. She wanted to switch careers, or at the very least to switch from her staff role to a position with line responsibility. But as an editorial director at a product goods company, she saw no way to make that kind of switch within her current company.

"Since I had been placed in this job through a headhunter, I thought that I would try that route again," she said. "Well, the recruiters I spoke to were certainly very willing to talk to me about positions in the same general area where I had worked before. They saw I had experience in internal communications, and so they called me about jobs in internal communications.

"But when I said what I was really interested in doing was making a switch—either a complete career switch or at the very least a switch from a staff role to direct line experience— they themselves acknowledged they could not help. They all told me that the client wanted a *proven* quantity, not a long shot. Unfortunately, that's just the way things are."

Stephanie B. eventually did succeed in making her career switch. But *not* through a headhunter.

4.

Having graduated from college with honors, Kathy B. began her hunt for a first job with great enthusiasm, only to become quickly disillusioned by the number of rejections she received. Frustrated, she sent resumes to agencies—executive-recruiting firms, of course, since she was determined to be an executive. When she received no response even to these letters, she called to discover what was causing the problem. "Ms. B., I think there's been a misunderstanding. What you're looking for is an employment agency," the secretary patiently explained to her. "Executive recruiters and employment agencies aren't the same at all."

5.

All through college and the first two years of graduate school, Susan S. had assumed she would pursue an academic career —until she realized, from the experience of her disgruntled older colleagues, that almost no university teaching jobs were to be had. She remembered meeting an executive recruiter at a cocktail reception once and decided to call. "How nice of you to remember me," the recruiter told her. "But really, you should be looking into one of those business recycling programs for Ph.D.s. Once you've made the transition and have some experience behind you, don't hesitate to call again."

The morals to these tales are short and sweet: The recruiter does not give career counseling. He cannot create or produce jobs on demand, nor does he run an employment agency. His office is not to be confused with a placement office for bright young graduates. And for executives contemplating a career change, he probably won't be very much help.

RECRUITERS AS CAREER RESOURCES

So what *can* an executive recruiter do for you?

If you think of recruiters as matchmakers, then you might also think of them as modern-day executive *yentas*. Like the know-it-all gossips of Yiddish tradition, they must make it their business to know about the companies and industries for which they recruit. They must have what every *yenta* needs and thrives on: information.

Thus, they make it their business to ferret out information about top-level management in their client companies, information about the middle managers whom they screen and interview, and information about jobs that could advance your career.

Besides information, they make it their business to possess that other golden commodity—access. Access to the client companies who are hiring. Access to the people who make decisions. And finally, access to you.

But how do you get access to them? How do you get the headhunter to hunt you? Why should you want a headhunter to call you? Some answers:

• A friendly headhunter may provide an iron in the fire when you need one.

• With so many mergers and acquisitions taking place, even if your current position is not in jeopardy now, there's no guarantee it won't be in the future.

• Further, as Chris Stevens, former national manager of consultants for Upjohn, asks, "Just how secure is your job, anyway? Who's to say that tomorrow your boss won't quit or the market won't change?"

• Because staying in one position or company too long may have an isolating effect, speaking to a headhunter may be a painless way to inform yourself of the range of other opportunities that exist, as well as to test yourself in the current marketplace.

• Speaking to a headhunter may also help those who work for large, highly structured organizations see what possibilities exist for finding a different career route within newer, smaller, less highly structured companies.

In short, the headhunter is someone who can keep your hat in the ring and keep you abreast of the marketplace; he is also someone to call upon and keep in touch with—just in case. For these reasons the career strategist will do well to cultivate at least one headhunter, and maybe more, as a career resource for the future.

ONE CAREER RESOURCE OR MANY?

Having said that the executive recruiter can be an excellent career resource, it may sound paradoxical to point out that he should be only *one* resource among many.

The reasoning is simple:

- Executive recruiters are not personal job counselors.
- They do not work for you; they are hired and paid by the client company.
- At the same time that they are calling you, they will be calling other potential candidates for the same job.
- A typical recruiter may work on from six to ten searches a year. The more recruiters you know, then, the better placed you will be to hear about and possibly be recruited for appropriate positions.

Who or what should your other career resources include?

First of all, the checklist should include your experience, education, and background. These are the actual *assets* you bring to a job.

But to whose attention do you wish to bring that very excellent portfolio? With whom—specifically with what company —do you wish to invest these assets? From whom could you learn about the existence of potential opportunities for investment at a higher growth rate than you might currently have?

Your initial checklist might run something like this:

- Colleagues and professional friends both within and outside your current company
- Professional or trade associations of which you are a member
- Alumnae/alumni associations
- Community groups with whom you are active
- Headhunters

As you can see, the headhunter is an excellent resource to have, but ideally he should be only one resource among many.

MANAGING—AND NOT MANAGING— YOUR CAREER

Ideally, your greatest resource should be yourself. After all, no one will know what you want from your career—and more important, from your life as a whole—if you do not. And to know yourself, you must evaluate yourself.

Well, it's easy to tell you to evaluate yourself, you say—all the advice books say it, so why shouldn't this one, too? But just how do you go about making this evaluation? And why bother?

"Many men and women, but especially women, I think, tend to be rather short-sighted about what a career really means," says Jeanne Marie Gilbert, a public relations/marketing consultant and former recruiter. "They don't necessarily understand you have to have a planned career, rather than just react to the jobs you happen to be in. And you really can't use headhunters properly until you look at yourself in that planned context."

Gilbert is not the only one who emphasizes the importance of looking at careers in this broader context. "Are women more unfocused than men in regard to their careers? Probably," says Martha Green, former director of career counseling at Barnard College. "Because they probably had a more interrupted and varied career, and so it seems less one-tracked. They also don't have a history of whole families of women who were in finance or a history of women who were lawyers."

Yet another socio-cultural element might be involved as well. "Women generally wait too long to act on their own behalf" when a job starts to go sour, comments Nella Barkley, president of the John C. Crystal Center in New York City, a leading career management and planning organization. "It is a characteristic that is very remarkable. It's a cultural thing, waiting to be asked," rather than actively taking charge and making things happen on one's own.

A number of recruiters, counselors, and executive women agree that if there is one difference between the way men and women view their careers, it is that when the current job becomes problematic, women tend to adopt a strategy that one might call the ostrich technique. Rather than stick their heads in the sand, however, they bury their noses in their in-boxes.

Certainly this tendency can be found in men as well as women. Denial is a universal method for coping with things that are just too difficult or painful to face. But perhaps, having fought so hard to break into high-level positions, it is that much more painful for many women to acknowledge that a particular situation just isn't working out.

"I knew that the new tax reforms were going to affect the real-estate business," an executive at a real estate investment firm says, "but I guess I didn't want to think about it. Now suddenly the company is in trouble, colleagues both at my own level and people even more senior are being forced out, and I don't know what to do. The headhunters have been nice, but I know I'm not the only one calling."

"Before I got my new job, I kept thinking it was me, not the job," a general counsel for a large utility company in the Northeast says. "I had to become very miserable before I finally realized there was something I could do about it."

"If there's one thing I learned," an executive at a computer firm confides, "it's that the more you keep your head down and worry about your own job, when you finally do lift your head up, you're not positioned, you're entrenched, people don't know what you're interested in doing next. I know. That's what happened to me."

The stages are common: a stubborn denial that something is amiss is followed by the gradual realization that it is time to move to another job. Unfortunately, by the time that stage is reached, the job may have grown so unbearable, and morale may have fallen so low, that the always difficult task of looking for something new may seem even more daunting.

Almost everyone has had at least one job that did not work out, and the reason behind leaving a job could be anything: your old boss changes jobs, and the new one wants to bring in his own staff; the company is bought, and everything is changing; an aggressive competitor cuts into the company's market, and you're among the ones laid off; the job does not turn out to be what you thought it would be, a promised promotion evaporates, or it's just plain time to move on.

Many of these circumstances are both unpredictable and unavoidable. However, there are certain warning signals:

- Rumors are afloat about a possible takeover or merger.
- The company stock continues to do poorly.
- The industry as a whole continues to do poorly.
- You are passed over for a promotion.
- Although you are asked to be the acting boss after a superior leaves, you are not given the position permanently.
- You are not invited to meetings, or included in decisions, of which you used to be a part.
- Your boss can no longer find time to talk to you.

It could happen to anyone. It could happen to you. And if it does? Do you deny it until it goes away? Take action? What kind of action?

The best solution is to take action long before these warnings begin. The prescription is simple—career planning. Nella Barkley calls it life planning. The phrase sounds intimidating until you break down the process, step by step. The first thing to do is to figure out where you are currently: How do you feel about your job, your life, yourself? Are you in a professional rut or at a career plateau? How do your careers goals fit in with more general goals for your life as a whole? Is your career window open or closed? What are the demons that drive you, professionally and personally? Where do you want them to drive you? And how will you get there?

WHERE YOU ARE NOW

You might begin by marking what Martha Green calls a "score-card of your life." Here are some items to consider in your satisfaction checklist:

1. *Are You Living to Work, or Working to Live?*
To love and to work, Freud said. But how do you wish to balance the two? How satisfied are you with the balance you are currently striking?
How happy are you with the way you spend the hours of your life? Are your work hours too strenuous? Not strenuous enough? Just right?

2. *Are You Working for Love or for Money?*
Money isn't everything, but your paycheck is one tangible piece of evidence of how you are valued by those who write the paychecks. It can also be a measure of how we see ourselves in relation to colleagues and contemporaries.
How much money do you earn, including your entire compensation package?
Is that enough?
If it isn't, does that matter?
Why or why not?
Are there other kinds of "psychic" income that matter as much, or more, to you—for example, the challenge involved, your love of the work itself, the sense that you are involved in meaningful work, the feeling that you work for an organization you believe in, the job's cachet, the publicity, the glamour, etc.?

3. *Are You Working for Status and Recognition?*
"I've had lots of jobs from which I got a lot of status at cocktail parties," Martha Green relates. "Political campaign jobs, for instance. But the fact of the matter was, the campaign management job was so difficult and the hours were so

strenuous that I hardly ever got to a cocktail party. So finally I
had to say, 'Hey, wait a minute! There's a long distance from
one cocktail party to the next, and is that enough?' "

Is it?

From whom do you want recognition? What are the
achievements that you would like recognition for?

From whom are you receiving recognition now? Your boss?
Colleagues? Friends? And for what, precisely, are you receiving
that recognition?

How much, at bottom, does recognition from others mean to
you? Why does it matter to you, or why does it not matter? If it
does not matter, what matters instead?

4.*What Does Your Inner Voice Say?*

The previous question covered external satisfactions—how
others regard you. But what about the way you regard
yourself?

In a society that places so much emphasis on material
success, the inner voice that reminds us of our ideals and
values can grow faint or even be lost. Is that happening to you?

What are the aspects of your current job that yield a sense of
inner satisfaction or accomplishment? Do you find your
current job lacking in these aspects? Are there other jobs in
which you think they would be present? What are they?

5. *Where You Work: How Would You Rate Your Job
Environment?*

Since we spend so many hours at work—working not only
in a specific place, but with specific people—it's important to
look at the human and cultural contexts in which we live the
hours of nine to five and longer each day.

How would you rate your relationships with:

Your colleagues?

Your subordinates?

Your boss?

Do you like the city where you work?

The office building?

The office in which you sit?

How would you describe the corporate culture of your company? Are you comfortable with it? If so, why? If not, why not?

6. Is It a Job, or Is It a Career?

"There are people who have a number of jobs but no career," explains Howard O. Williams, Jr., Ph.D., president of the New York-based outplacement firm of Howard Williams Associates. "These are people who don't think about how their careers fit together as a whole. They've got a little bit of personnel, some strategic planning, some line experience, and so on. They're just all over the place." But the key to planning a career is putting all these different experiences together as a coherent whole.

So ask yourself the following questions:

How do all the jobs or positions you've ever held fit together? What are the common threads in terms of both interests and achievements? (Having no pattern is also a pattern.)

Where do you see this pattern leading you next?

Ideally, where would you like it to lead you?

Practically speaking, where will it lead you?

Is there room for advancement where you are now?

If not, do you see any logical next steps at other companies?

Do you *want* to advance?

If so, why? And where?

If not, why not?

7. Oh, How I Love (Hate) To Get Up in the Morning!

Energy derives from enthusiasm and excitement. How much energy do you have to contribute to your current job? How do you feel each morning when you cross your office threshold? What are your emotions telling you about the job itself?

Do you love, hate, or feel indifferent toward the work you face each morning?

Do you feel appreciated, a contributor to the company effort?

Or do you feel underpaid, underappreciated, and understimulated?

To all of these questions—why or why not?

8. If There Is One Thing I Would Change...

Nothing in life is perfect. Even the best job must carry with it occasional frustrations and disappointments. And so if there is one thing you would change:

about your job...

about your career...

about your life...

What would that one thing be?

If there are other things that you would change, what would they be? How much are you bothered by the factors you have listed? Enough to make a change? If so, what kind of change?

9. If There Is One Thing I Would Not Change...

It is equally important to evaluate those aspects of your job that matter to you the most. What are the qualities, aspects, or factors that make you feel good when you think:

about your job...

about your career...

about your life...

The more things you list the better. If you can't think of much to recommend any of these aspects of your life, however, then perhaps it's time to evaluate even further why you are where you are now.

10. Overall, How Would You Rate Your Ratings?

Perhaps the most difficult part of the self-assessment exercise comes next. It is realizing that no one can evaluate your scorecard for you. You must score the answers according to your own highly personal, internal system of values.

Begin by summing up your answers so far:

Were your comments about your job weighted more heavily toward the positive or the negative side of the scale?

Were your comments about your career more positive or negative?

Were your comments about the other aspects of your life more positive or negative?

If everything was positive—terrific! You have found an excellent comfort level in both your career and in your life as a whole. You have found the right balance for you.

If you found yourself in the middle—as most people do—then this test has served as the first step toward helping you identify those aspects of your work life that give you the greatest satisfaction, as well as the particular factors that grate on you. Your next step is twofold: first, to see if there are ways to fine-tune what is good already; second, to explore possible changes that might make a difference in tipping the balance even further toward the positive side of the scale.

If you found yourself grumbling about everything all the way through this exercise, then the time is probably long overdue to identify some very concrete ways of changing those things that cause the greatest difficulty and discomfort.

PEAK, VALLEY, OR PLATEAU?

Before further evaluating where you want to go in the future, let's look for a moment at where you stand now. Are you at a peak, in a valley, or at a plateau? To locate your position, answer the following twelve questions:

1. Were you promoted recently?
2. Have you been passed over for a promotion recently?
3. Do you communicate well with your superiors? Receive feedback when you ask for it? Receive positive and constructive performance reviews?
4. Has your boss learned to rely on you more and more as you worked together, or has he become less open with you recently?
5. If your boss left or went on a leave of absence, would you be promoted? Asked to take on the temporary responsibility of

becoming the acting boss? What would your chances be of subsequently being offered that or an equivalent position?

6. Do colleagues at the same level appear to be moving ahead at a pace faster, slower, or at about the same rate as you?

7. When you look up the ladder at your present company, is there a rung for you?

8. Is it a rung that you both want to reach and conceivably could reach?

9. Are there so many people vying for that single rung that the odds of your reaching it are even at best?

10. Is there no rung for you even if you did want to move up within the company?

11. If you are not interested regardless of the chances, why not?

12. All things considered, after answering these questions, would you regard yourself as being at a peak, a plateau, or in a valley at your current position?

HAVING DISCOVERED WHERE YOU ARE NOW...

What's next? Put all the answers into the broader context of what you want to do with your life.

"We never concentrate on what people call career planning," Nella Barkley says. "Our first question is never: What kind of work do you want? It's: How do you want to live your life?"

It's a matter of putting first things first, she explains: "Because if people can figure out how they want to live their lives, then they can proceed to get the kind of work that will enable them to live those kinds of lives."

Only in this way—by looking at your career within the broader context of your life as a whole—will you find the best next step to your career, Barkley and other career counselors believe. Why? For one thing, taking the broad view may help you to clarify why you have made certain choices, as well as help crystallize what you would prefer to be doing instead.

"People sometimes think that the next step in a career is always the next step up the ladder," Barkley points out, "but they can't provide a rationale beyond prestige and dollars." If those are the only things you're after, fine. But it's important to remember that the obvious next step for someone else won't necessarily be the best one for you. Further, forced fits don't fool anyone for long—not your boss and certainly not yourself.

But what would that better fit be? What would be the best fit? How do you tailor your career to your own goals and capabilities?

SO WHAT'S YOUR LIFE STORY?

One way to find the best pattern for that fit is to look at the pattern of your life so far.

"Take a good hard look at your own history," Barkley counsels, "because the secrets of most of our capacities are hiding in what we've demonstrated."

Indeed, many career counselors advise writing an autobiography—a personal narrative of your achievements and accomplishments. This would include what you've enjoyed doing, what you've hated doing, the challenges you've overcome, where and how you've lived your life and why.

Writing this sort of narrative need not be daunting, and it need not adhere to a particular form. Career counselors themselves offer different suggestions for writing your life story. Richard Bolles, author of *What Color Is Your Parachute*, advises keeping the work as informal as possible and stresses the unstructured nature of the task. You're not writing for publication, after all, but for yourself.

But in their career handbook, *What to Do With the Rest of Your Life*, the staff members of Catalyst, a highly regarded national nonprofit organization for women, present a highly structured questionnaire and suggest writing a lengthy, detailed analysis.

In fact, there are probably as many ways to complete this exercise as there are individual life stories to tell. But whether you choose to set down your life history as an impressionistic diary or begin by systematically listing all the facts of your life, one piece of advice remains constant: be as specific as possible.

- Be specific about your *achievements:* on the job, at home, in your spare time.
- Be specific about what you *enjoyed* in accomplishing those things. Was it the goal, the activity itself, the place, the people, the recognition that resulted, or a combination of the above?
- Be specific about what you did *not* enjoy and why.

Once you have written your narrative, read it and analyze it as carefully as you would a novel for a literature course. What patterns do you see? What are the recurring themes? What can you discover from all these specific facts about the patterns of your life as a whole:

- Patterns of interests
- Patterns of tasks or activities that you dislike
- Patterns of values that matter to you
- Patterns of skills
- Patterns of working that help you achieve at the highest levels
- Patterns of working that lead to lower levels of achievement

The more specific you are, the better able you will be to identify what you want from your career, the better position you will be in to manage your career, and the better prepared you will be to use all the different resources for career advancement.

WHAT ARE THE DEMONS THAT DRIVE YOU? (AND WHERE ARE THEY DRIVING YOU?)

Nella Barkley points out that executive recruiters will some-times suggest that candidates speak to career counselors *before* coming to see them. Why? "These are excellent candidates who don't come across as fully focused because they really don't know what they want."

And if you don't know what you want from your job or career, how can the recruiter?

What *do* you want? What makes you tick? What are the demons that drive you? Where do you *want* them to drive you?

Here are some more suggestions to help you discover the answers:

1. *Read all the newspapers and magazines you can get your hands on, but read them in a different way.*

a. Read the obituaries. This suggestion might sound morbid, until you consider what you can learn from the life histories of others: "You see that great people didn't say in fifth grade, 'I love math and therefore I'm going to become the best accountant in the world!'" points out Kathleen Lusk Brooke, director of the Center for the Study of Success in Boston. "Their lives and interests were much more varied. They combined things in different ways." In considering what worked for them, think about the combinations that work best for you.

b. Read the classifieds. What turns you on or off? What are the different combinations of experience that you have to offer that others might be looking for? What kinds of experience are you lacking that *would* put you in the running for something you want?

c. Read the paper as a personal fantasy land. "I tell people to save up the papers for a week or two," Brooke says, "then flip through page after page very quickly. Clip out every article or ad or photograph or headline that your eyes light on for more than a glance. Then sort those clippings into piles based on where they seem to fall. And hard as it may be to believe, they *will* fall into piles or categories, usually between two to five of them. These will tell you what your interests are"—and hint at roles you would like to see yourself playing in the future.

2. *Find out what demons drive your friends.*

   a. What do your friends who enjoy their jobs enjoy about them? What do they hate about them? What lessons about your own likes and dislikes can you learn from theirs? Perhaps you're griping about something that *everyone* in a particular profession must learn to live with if he wishes to stay in that profession. Or perhaps you've been blaming yourself for not liking a job that, objectively speaking, is so problematic that *no one* could like it.

   b. "Look at everyone you know or know about, even if it's just from the evening news, and see if there's anyone you'd like to be," Brooke suggests. "Those are not necessarily lives that will be available to you, but there may be important seeds there," whether in terms of role models or suggested paths and possibilities.

   c. Cultivate the habit of *listening*. Often listening to others talk about themselves—their own hopes, goals, and disappointments—can help clarify and crystallize your own feelings.

3. *Get feedback about yourself:*

   a. "Go to an executive training course," suggests Howard O. Williams, Jr. Such programs frequently provide the opportunity for you to get feedback from others regarding not just your job skills, but your interpersonal abilities. Such feedback can offer insight about how others actually see you; alas, this vision won't always mesh with how you *want* others to see you! The lessons learned can help you to polish those rough edges. As you do so, you might also find you are starting to come across better to—and get along better with—colleagues, subordinates, and superiors.

b. Have you ever noticed how your friends sometimes seem to know you better than you do yourself? "Talk to three people who know you fairly well and also know the world," Brooke advises. "Say to them, 'Knowing all you do, where would you see me?'" Use their perceptions of your abilities, aspirations, and weaknesses as a means of learning how others view you—and of what other possibilities might exist for you.

IS YOUR CAREER WINDOW OPEN OR CLOSED?

Let's say you have just received a recruiter's phone call. How would you respond? How would you have responded to each of the calls described at the start of this chapter? Would you have been open or closed to their suggestions for change? Why or why not? How would you respond now?

I would suggest that simply listening carefully to these callers may tell you more about yourself than you suspect, for in deciding whether or not you are interested in what the caller has to offer, you are also answering many of the questions posed earlier in this chapter: Are you happy or dissatisfied with your current position? What elements would encourage you to make a change? What factors about your present situation could never be improved upon, no matter what someone else's offer might be? One of the most positive things a recruiter's phone call can do is help you to articulate what is right—and what is wrong—with where you are now and what aspects in *any* position would or would not attract your attention.

A headhunter's phone call will often prompt an executive to start that process. What happened to Wendy Crisp in the anecdote related earlier in this chapter, for instance, is not at all uncommon. "When you contact someone who is happily employed and never thought about leaving, I would say that within six months that person will have made a job change," says Janet Jones-Parker, executive director of the Association of Executive Search Consultants.

A headhunter's call can do that, but you should not wait for it. Think through your goals and know what you want even before the headhunter calls. "Know who you are and where you are going," Jones-Parker counsels.

After all, the more focused your goals and motivations are the better prepared you will be to plan what comes next in the context of both your career and, more important, of your life as a whole. You'll be prepared to make better, more well-informed decisions—and not only when the recruiter calls.

Of course, regardless of how much information you gather about yourself, none of it will do you any good at all unless you're willing to analyze and use it. Similarly, it's so easy to get so mired in the daily routine of our lives that we forget the larger goals or plans we had set out to follow long ago. These exercises were designed to help you think through those goals and plans once more—to help you focus not only on hunting a headhunter, but also on defining what it is you want. Now that you have thought these things through, we are ready to move on.

2

WHO'S DOING THE HUNTING?

SOME HEADHUNTERS ARE INTRODUCED

As in every profession, headhunters come in every variety imaginable: elitists and mass marketers, sympathetic nurturers and friendly listeners, chatty salespeople and cold-eyed business folk. And as in every profession, too, among them you will find the good, the wonderful, the bad, and the awful.

Here are a few of the diverse types I came across in my research, and that you may encounter in your interviews:

1.

Some recruiters cringe at the term "headhunter." Others shrug their shoulders and live with it. But perhaps no one flaunts the term with more panache than Allan D. R. Stern, chairman of Haskell and Stern Associates, one of the more distinguished firms in New York, as he waves a visitor into his elegant office and nonchalantly points to two strikingly ugly shrunken heads—tiny, withered, clay-colored grimaces framed by dark black hair. They are clearly out of place here, amidst the brightly colored paintings, the Steuben glass, the mahogany desk, and comfortable English-style furniture.

Lean and tall, with thinning brown hair and clear blue eyes,

Stern lights a cigarette and smiles. "We're ivory hunters rather than headhunters, I like to say."

And quite right, too, you think. This is a gentleman you're speaking to, not a savage. Now some parts of corporate America may be jungles, but certainly not this office! An executive recruiter like Allan Stern a headhunter? How on earth could anyone ever confuse the two?

2.

And you feel much the same way as you enter another Manhattan skyscraper, just a few blocks away.

This is the view from the fortieth floor: you stare at the glorious skyline, and the glass office towers glare back, while the metal spires of Midtown Manhattan gleam in the midday sun.

Then you move from the window and focus instead on the tall, slim figure before you. She is dressed in beige and gray. Her high cheekbones give way to a cautious, understated smile, and as she grasps your hand in greeting, you are suddenly at ease. Yet whether she is speaking or listening, leaning back in her chair, or edging forward with tapered fingers resting on her chin, you cannot escape the sense that it is you who are the center of attention here.

You are being interviewed by Jean Boler of Handy Associates, one of the largest and most prestigious of recruiting firms, and everything is so perfectly well mannered and calm that you sense you have entered a special world here—the world of the *crème de la crème*, the world of the fortieth floor.

3.

And now we go to another firm on another street—and a different world entirely. The waiting room walls are white and blank. On the radiator beside the single sofa lies a well-worn copy of *Working Woman*. As you wait for the receptionist to notice you, you can't help but overhear the conversation in the conference room down the hall:

"So you call and identify yourself, give your name and the company's name, and then you say, 'I'm calling to introduce myself and my firm and to find out a little bit about your background. Do you have a minute?'"

"Yeah, yeah. Then what?"

"All right. You describe the job. 'I'm currently working on a situation for one of my clients in e.d.p., and it was recommended to me that you were in that area—'"

"Wait a second—e.d.p.? What's that? You know I'm not familiar with this industry."

"Electronic data processing. I'll explain in a minute—I'll go over all the terms you'll need to know, don't worry. But first, let me go over what you want to find out."

You peek behind the reception desk and see a long, carpeted room filled with two long rows of desks. At each desk, people are sitting with telephones glued to their ears. Above the cacophonous chatter, you begin to recognize the words as part of a familiar chorus, "Hello, my name is . . . I'm currently working on a situation for one of my clients. Do you have a minute?"

And what you've just heard in the conference room down the hall, you realize, is the *training* session for one of the recruiters who might well soon be calling you—one of many, many people they'll be calling to fill one of their client's positions. You listen some more, and you begin to wonder whom they *wouldn't* call. . . .

And you think: If you're looking for a *head*hunter, you've found one.

4.

Next we visit still another type of recruiter. You walk through the wrought-iron gate and the inner courtyard beyond and wonder at the peculiar calm on this side street on the East Side of Manhattan. At the sound of the buzzer, you pass through the door, climb the steep flight of stairs to another door, and are greeted there not by someone in a gray flannel suit, but by a young woman in corduroy slacks and a velour sweater casually cradling her two-year-old son in her arms.

"Oh, come on in—excuse us—we're just finishing up here," another woman says, this one in an elegantly informal camel-colored dress, as she helps the other to fold up the blue and yellow blankets, the colorful blocks, a stray toy here and there.

The offices of Kanarek and Shaw are small and cluttered. A desk stacked with papers is tucked against one wall; bookshelves overflow with heavy volumes bound in red and green and black. At the far end of the room are two somewhat worn green sofas and a coffee table. All in all, the setting may well remind you of a well-to-do graduate student's living room. Instinctively, you feel at home here; this is not the setting for an interview, but for a comfortable chat.

"I'm a legal recruiter," Carol Kanarek says, and "No, I don't cold-call people"—that is, go down a list of associates in a law firm and give them a pitch about a wonderful-sounding opportunity. "But I do talk to everyone who calls me. We take a different approach here—a more personal one. Well—more like matchmaking," she says. "Making a good fit."

5.

"We're basically harmless people," says the next recruiter we meet. He is Howard W. Stevens, an affable, gray-haired partner at the Bankers Register, a firm specializing in the financial industry. Smiling warmly, he adds, "We're like the matchmaker in *Fiddler on the Roof*."

And you certainly feel at ease here. The small conference room where you meet has a comfortable personality of its own: Decorating the walls are a series of antique postcards showing turn-of-the-century bank buildings in Milwaukee, Buffalo, New York, and Boston. A bookshelf holds other treasures—a banking directory from about the same period, and an old fashioned metal penny savings bank in the shape of a freight train car.

All this is certainly welcoming. And yet the waiting room outside possesses at least one of the trappings associated with an employment agency: the anxious young job candidate sitting there, filling out forms, "registering" with the firm.

And it's true, Stevens openly admits, that the Bankers Register might be best described as a full-service executive-recruiting firm, handling everything from high-level secretarial positions to executive positions at the middle-management and senior levels. For those seeking lower-level positions, the firm might be viewed as an employment agency; in fact, Stevens says, state regulations at one point required them to register as one. But that is only one aspect of the firm's business. It is also a respected contingency search firm, and it occasionally handles retained searches as well.

And so you nod in agreement when he repeats, "We're basically harmless people." Yes, he admits, there are some firms that give the industry a bad name—that's true of every industry or profession. But listening to Stevens's friendly baritone voice, you can't help but be sympathetic as he wonders aloud, Why are so many executives both fearful and skeptical of the executive recruiting profession?

THE INDUSTRY SURVEYED

As these brief portraits demonstrate, recruiters wear all manner of faces. They project different voices, possess different styles, and work in different ways. But they are all recruiters nonetheless.

The industry is large and varied. Here is an overview to guide you through it.

How Old Is Headhunting?

Not very. The executive-recruiting business is relatively new and still growing. Although Thorndike Deland Associates, still one of New York's best-known retainer firms, was founded in 1926, in this business an "old" firm seems to mean one that was founded before 1960. Indeed, the two largest American firms in terms of revenues, Korn/Ferry International and Russell Reynolds, did not open their doors until 1969, and James Kennedy, editor and publisher of *Executive Recruiter News*, estimates that more than 90 percent of all contingency and retainer firms have been founded since the 1960s.

The industry's growth in the last decade has been impressive. "The average total revenue growth among the Big Six firms over the last four years has been an astounding 110 percent," *Fortune*[1] declared in 1981. In 1983, industry figures showed a 20 percent increase over 1982, *Time*[2] duly reported. And another 20 percent increase in revenues was reported between 1984 and 1985, according to *The New York Times*.[3]

Without question, the growth has been substantial; not only have the older firms flourished, but newer firms are cropping up all the time. Recruiters from the larger firms often leave to form firms of their own, and many people from outside the industry are drawn to the profession by the seeming promise of dramatic growth and large profits:

"'Recruit' yourself into one of the most profitable and exciting industries," reads the description for a course sponsored by New York's Learning Annex. "'Head-hunting' firms have evolved into a highly professional and respected industry. Executive searchers make *lots* of money filling the personnel needs of companies, large and small." For twenty-one dollars, the brochure promises, the three-hour course, given by the founders of a highly successful contingency firm specializing in the computer industry, will "show you step-by-step everything you need to know."

Really? The hype is so seductive, no wonder so many new firms open—and also fail. Kenneth Cole, publisher of *Recruit-*

---

[1]"Headhunters Cast a Wider Net," *Fortune*, September 7, 1981.

[2]"Invasion of the Body Snatchers," *Time*, April 23, 1984.

[3]*The New York Times*, August 10, 1986.

ing and Search Report, estimates that for every recruiting firm in the business today there is at least another one that has both entered and left the field since 1980, the year he first started tracking the industry. "The turnover is incredible," he says.

That's not to say that a new firm won't last. But it does provide a reason to ask how long the firm and the recruiter, who may have branched off on his own after working for many years at other firms, have been in business before you send in your resume.

The industry has grown so rapidly, in fact, that some recruiters are predicting a shakeup. With so much competition, they warn, it is the larger, well-established firms and the smaller specialty firms that will remain the most viable, with mid-sized firms that don't specialize falling by the wayside.

"Headhunters face off in shootout as search industry consolidates," the headline in Crain's New York Business ran.[4] Allan Stern, for one, agrees that, "The big growth is going to be in the smaller and medium-sized firms." John Dugan, chairman of the National Association of Executive Recruiters and himself a recruiter specializing in the plastics industry, points to "a continued demand and increase in specialization" among firms.

These trends will be considered further later in this chapter as factors to be weighed when deciding which firms you as a candidate may wish to contact.

HEADHUNTERS VS. EMPLOYMENT AGENCIES

"Headhunters and employment agencies—aren't they the same thing?" people often ask. "Isn't executive recruiter just a fancy name for someone in personnel?"

Well, headhunters may get huffy when the comparison is made, but there are a number of similarities:

---

[4]Crain's New York Business, October 13, 1986.

- Search firms and employment agencies both deal in job placements.
- Search firm fees are always paid by the employer; employment agency fees are usually paid by the employer as well.
- All employment agencies work on a contingency basis; that is, they are paid only if they fill a position. Many recruiting firms also work on contingency. (For more on contingency vs. retainer firms, see page 64.)
- Employment agencies usually handle secretarial and junior-level positions. But there are also contingency-recruiting firms that, in addition to higher-level positions, handle jobs at the lower end of the market.

"Employment agencies are operating at the bread-and-butter level," comments Kathleen Lusk Brooke, director of the Boston-based Center for the Study of Success. "They're asking, 'Do you want to make $100 more a week?'" Alas, some recruiting firms have been known to make similar pitches in only slightly different words!

Those are the similarities. But there are also a number of important—and to the job seeker, crucial—differences:

- Executive-search firms *never* charge the candidate a fee; their fees are paid by the client company. Some employment agencies are paid a percentage of the job seeker's salary by the job seeker himself.
- Executive-search firms work for the client company. They do not represent the job candidate, nor can they be "hired" by a job seeker to find a job. By contrast, employment agencies will market the job seeker as part of their wares; in that sense, they may be seen as representing or acting as a kind of agent for the job seeker.
- Executive-search firms may occasionally advertise for *specific* jobs they are seeking to fill. On the other hand, employment agencies advertise frequently, at times for jobs that don't exist as a ploy to get people in the door.

- Executive-search firms handle executive and management positions, many at the highest level. Employment agencies generally handle openings at a lower level of responsibility, often at the entry level or just above.
- Executive-search firms often work on *retainer;* that is, they are paid by the client company whether they succeed in filling the position or not. Employment agencies work exclusively on contingency. (See Contingency Vs. Retainer Firms, page 64.)

HEADHUNTERS VS. CAREER COUNSELORS

Executive-recruiting firms are not the same as employment agencies. Nor are they to be confused with career counselors.

True, at times executive recruiters may provide some free advice. And some will offer professional career counseling on the side, for a set fee. For instance, Sydney Reynolds, president of the New York-based firm Sydney Reynolds Associates, says, "I'm not in the business of counseling, and I don't engage in it a lot." But on those few occasions when she does agree to act as a career counselor rather than as a recruiter, her fee is $150 an hour. For the most part, however, recruiters are just that—recruiters.

Career counselors, by contrast, are in the business of advising job seekers, career changers, people who want to define or refine what comes next in their lives. That is their business and that is what they will charge you for.

Who should consult a career counselor?

Certainly not everyone needs formal career counseling. Often you can fine-tune your future plans or crystallize what it is you're seeking by yourself, following the kinds of self-assessment exercises provided in Chapter One and in a number of books on the market today. But there are also times when an outside perspective is precisely what you need. In those cases, a career counselor can assist in:

- Assessing what is and is not working in your career now.
- Helping you plan what you really want to do with your career.
- Advising you on what steps to take to get you there.
- Opening your eyes to opportunities you may not have been able to see on your own.

Career counselors, in short, can act as both adviser and coach as you go about deciding what comes next.

There are also times when a recruiter will refer a job candidate to a career counselor, says Nella Barkley, the career counselor, particularly when the recruiter thinks that the job seeker "is somehow coming across unfocused because he doesn't really know what he wants."

Career counselors come in many varieties. They may offer individual counseling, group counseling, psychological testing, vocational testing, workshops on different aspects of the job hunt, library resources, job referrals, or some combination of the above.

There are many excellent bona fide counselors, but beware. Some counselors more closely resemble packagers, Kathleen Lusk Brooke warns, with the "package" costing between fifteen hundred and three thousand dollars or more. And what do you get for your money? "Basically, they rewrite your resume, give you coaching, videotape work, and hand you a telephone book," she says.

Rather than pay your money in one lump sum, find a private career counselor with whom you can pay as you go, Brooke advises. That way, she says, "If you see after the second session that it's going nowhere, you can drop it. But if you pay three thousand dollars up front, that's it."

Also beware of career counselors who promise to absolutely, positively find you a job. Can *anyone* truthfully make that promise? Yet some executives, vulnerable at the prospect of losing a job, may find themselves easy prey for such marketing tactics.

To find the career counseling you need, shop around. Have

any of your friends used career counselors? What were their experiences? Can they recommend anyone? Find out what your local college or your alumni association offers. Catalyst, the national clearinghouse for career information for women, publishes a directory of affiliated career counselors located throughout the country. See what your local YWCA or other community organizations might offer.

Or, if you find yourself already out of a job, your company might have referred you to the next option: outplacement.

HEADHUNTERS VS. OUTPLACEMENT SERVICES

Outplacement is the one benefit no executive wants to use. It is the counseling service provided to the fired executive to help him find a new position somewhere else.

Outplacement provides an extremely useful service, helping executives who may not have had to look for a new job for years to figure out how to take the next step at a most vulnerable point in their lives.

The company doing the firing will usually pay the outplacement fees. Nonetheless, the counselor should be seen as the job-hunter's advocate—a professional who will help counsel the executive in finding a new job, often employing many of the same techniques that a career counselor might.

"Ten years ago, outplacement was a matter of helping people to learn how to get a job," explains Howard O. Williams, Jr., Ph.D., president of the New York-based outplacement firm, Howard Williams Associates. "That meant you helped people put a resume together, send letters, and use a network. . . . Now outplacement is teaching and counseling—and actually doing part of the work, giving people contacts as well."

And who are some of the contacts that outplacement counselors like Williams will advise the job candidate to write? Headhunters, of course.

"It used to be a search firm would never talk to an outplacement firm," Williams continues. "But that has changed. We will get a number of calls from very good search firms saying, 'We know the kind of work you do. If you have people coming through [in whom our clients might be interested], if you could refer them to us, we would be very happy.' So outplacement is becoming another source for recruiters."

Although a number of recruiters still tend to be wary of outplacement firms (and "outplaced" people), some are more receptive than others—especially *after* the job seeker has received counseling and has focused his or her search.

CONTINGENCY FIRMS VS. RETAINER FIRMS

Contingency or retainer, what's the difference?

On the most basic level, the difference has only to do with how each type of firm is paid for its services:

- Retainer firms are hired (that is, retained) by client companies and paid for the services provided *whether or not the firm actually succeeds in filling the position.*
- Contingency firms are paid by a client company *only if and when the firm succeeds in filling the position.*

Now that may sound simple enough, but the question of whether to use a contingency or a retainer firm often draws fire. As one executive explains, "Contingency is like body-pushing; retainer is like shoulder-tapping."

Janet Jones-Parker, executive director of the Association of Executive Search Consultants, a professional association whose membership consists only of retainer firms, goes further: "A contingency agency is just a glorified employment agency," she says. "Contingency firms and employment agencies market people, not situations. An executive-search firm markets situations. That's the difference."

"I'll stand up for the contingency folks," says Kenneth Cole, publisher of the *Recruiting and Search Report.* "The trouble is that [the retainer agencies] don't differentiate between the employment agency and contingent search. There is a very big difference. I believe that whether the bill is paid now or later does not drive the quality of the search work. There are some excellent contingent-search firms."

Let's look into the differences—real and perceived—between these two types of firms in more detail:

Since they will be paid whether or not they fill a position, retainer firms say they can afford to devote more time and resources to a particular search than contingency firms. Contingency firms counter by saying that since their candidates are their products, they must work just as hard researching the candidates' backgrounds.

Nonetheless, contingency recruiters themselves admit that spending too long on a search that doesn't pan out simply isn't cost effective. And since they are paid only if they do fill a position, critics contend, contingency firms may want to fill that position as quickly as possible—sometimes whether it's the best offer for the job seeker or not.

But retained recruiters want to get on to the next search, too, contingency recruiters point out. And since a recruiter—whether he's contingency or retainer—thrives on repeat business from a client, a good recruiter will always try to find the best fit possible for both the client and the job seeker, regardless of the payment schedule.

Some contingency firms are said to send resumes en masse to potential client companies. Indeed, one executive complained to me that her resume had "accidentally" found its way from the headhunter's desk to the head of personnel at a subsidiary of her current company. Executives on the hiring end tell stories of receiving the same person's resume from more than one recruiter. Kenneth Cole, however, feels that in general there are many more apocryphal horror stories than there are actual cases of this sort of thing happening.

Client companies tend to hire retainer agencies for higher-level positions. As a result, most retainer firms will not look at candidates making under $50,000, and some will not even deal with people whose salaries fall below $75,000.

Contingency firms, however, tend to handle lower- or middle-level management positions. They frequently consider people making $30,000; some start as low as $20,000. Many companies will have several contingency firms working on a single search at the same time. Since they only pay if the position is filled, the rationale goes, the more recruiters they have searching on their behalf the more likely they will be to find a better candidate. For you as a job seeker, this means that if you've spoken to more than one contingency firm, theoretically *all* of them could send your resume to a single employer who then might wonder just how selective—and how desperate—you are. This does happen. But depending on your qualifications, the executive reading your multiple resumes, and the reputation of the firms who have sent them, this may not count as a mark against you.

By contrast, because of the costs involved, client companies generally hire only one retainer firm to conduct a search. As a result, you will not be in danger of having two recruiters submit your resume for the same job.

The bad news, then, is that some high-volume contingency firms can make you feel as if you are so much fodder for a hungry body-processing machine. Hard-driving recruiters may try to sell you on a particular position, which may not be right for you, in order to make the sale. Unscrupulous firms may also paper the industry with your resume.

But though retainer firms may have it all over the contingency firms in terms of snob appeal, that very snobbery can screen you out as a candidate. If you have not yet reached the level of job responsibility their clients require, these recruiters may make you feel as if you are the lowest of the low, unworthy of their attention or acknowledgment.

The good news, though, is that there are excellent, hardworking recruiters in both contingency and retainer firms.

Should you prefer one type of firm to another?

To some extent, the type of firm you choose will depend on the level of job responsibility you have reached. If you can work successfully with both types of firms, doing so may broaden the number of potential job opportunities that come your way.

Should you worry more about using a contingency firm than a retainer firm?

"A headhunter has very few assets, and the only real asset is his reputation," Kenneth Cole points out. "It takes a number of years to create a reputation of confidentiality and only a few seconds to blow that away. My sense is that most recruiters, retained and contingent both, will guard that confidentiality like the crown jewels."

Further, the distinctions between a retainer and a contingency firm aren't always clear. Some firms handle both types of searches. And there is also something called "exclusive contingency." In this case, the recruiter will work on contingency, but only that recruiter (or his firm) will be handling the assignment for a given period of time. If the recruiter does not fill the position within that time limit, other firms may be given the assignment as well.

However, since more could conceivably go awry when working with a contingency firm, check its reputation thoroughly, and make sure that the recruiter agrees not to send your resume anywhere without your approval.

SPECIALTY FIRMS

In a world of specialists, the executive-recruiting industry also has become increasingly specialized. In part, this trend has to do with the increasing number of firms. Rather than cast a net over several industries, many firms have found it both more productive and more profitable to focus on either a specific industry (health care or banking, for instance) or a particular function within the business sector as a whole (human resources, accounting, etc.). The firms are often small, sometimes with only one or two principal recruiters. Such firms can be either retainer or contingency.

Are there any advantages to working with a specialty firm? Because they concentrate on one particular industry or function, recruiters at these firms tend to know more about a particular field, to have more "insider" information, and to be more aware of and sensitive to the conditions under which you and the client company will best be able to work and thrive.

And companies who are in the market to hire an industry specialist often will go to a recruiting firm that specializes in their industry: "I find it more comfortable to work with the recruiter who specializes because that person will have experience in the field," says the director of placement and college relations at one of the nation's largest insurance companies.

However, recruiters with special expertise in a particular function or industry do not work only for specialty firms. You also will find many specialists working in larger, "generalist" firms, where they handle searches at the same level as or higher than those of the smaller specialty firms.

BIG FIRMS VS. SMALL FIRMS

In the world of executive recruiting, is small or big more beautiful?

The largest retainer firms, such as Korn/Ferry and Russell Reynolds, claim multimillion dollar yearly revenues, are international in scope with numerous offices around the globe, and employ large staffs of recruiters and researchers. They possess the capacity to fill far more openings in a given year than a smaller firm with only one or two principals operating on a less grandiose budget. Large firms also generally have the resources to run far more sophisticated research operations than smaller firms. Once your name finds its way into such a firm's computerized data bank, your resume becomes part of the research data base for all the recruiters in that firm.

But as they fill positions for more clients, large firms may also find more companies (or specified divisions or business units of companies) off limits to them. This is how it happens: Recruiters and clients agree in advance that once the search has been completed, employees of the client company as a whole, or a business unit or division of that company, will be off limits for that recruiter and his firm for a certain period of time, generally about two years. Smaller firms may handle fewer searches overall, but fewer companies will also be off limits to them.

Companies who are hiring a recruiter to fill a position will want to review this issue carefully. They must know, from the start, what companies the recruiter cannot tap, and how this will affect his ability to find the best person for the job.

But if you are a job candidate, and a recruiter is handling a search that interests you, it should not matter to you whether he is working with a large or a small firm. Unless, that is, you are a potential candidate, working for a company that is off limits to the recruiter. In that case, the ethical recruiter cannot present you as a candidate.

Those are the trade-offs. The key is to identify the recruiter within the search firm, large or small, handling searches in your industry or area of expertise.

WHATEVER HAPPENED TO THE "WOMEN ONLY" FIRMS?

In the early 1970s, as more women and minority group members entered the work force and as pressure was brought to bear to comply with equal-opportunity regulations, a new breed of headhunter was born: the recruiter who specialized in placing women and members of minority groups.

Sydney Reynolds, for instance, specialized in placing women executives from 1972 to 1975. In 1973, Janet Jones-Parker and Anne Hyde founded Management Woman, Inc. And about the same time Lynn Gilbert and Janet Tweed opened their firm, Gilbert Tweed Associates.

"At that time," Reynolds explains, "women were just entering the professional work force, the ERA was getting some teeth, women had fewer opportunities and they were easier to reach. But as the opportunities for women became abundant, there was less need [for companies] to have help in finding women in particular."

Indeed, by about 1982, the need for special firms concentrating on placing women had ended, Jones-Parker notes. Not only had many more women—a good many with newly earned MBAs—entered the work force and at ever higher levels, but EEOC pressures had begun to lighten. Further, Jones-Parker says, women "were no longer seen as 'troublemakers' pressuring their companies. Instead, they were concentrating on getting the expertise to advance and capture the opportunities that were available."

These days, recruiters say, firms still occasionally receive a request specifically for a woman candidate—particularly for a woman to sit on a board of directors. But Management Woman, Inc. ceased to exit in 1982, and Sydney Reynolds, Gilbert Tweed, and other firms that once specialized in placing women have long since abandoned that label.

The new emphasis these days is on finding the best candidate for the job. Period. And if a firm claims to take "special interest" in handling women, you may well take a moment to ask the recruiter what that means.

SHOULD A WOMAN SEEK OUT WOMEN RECRUITERS?

"No," Janet Jones-Parker answers succinctly. "In fact, most women recruiters probably avoid recruiting women because they want to avoid that label."

"It's not that they don't want to help other women," she emphasizes. "It's a business issue. If I'm a purple person and I want to be a success in business and not just a segment of that business, then it's best that I avoid recruiting purple people because the assumption is, 'Well, you're purple, therefore you can recruit purple people.'"

And so a recruiter who happens to be female will not necessarily be a better—or a worse—recruiter for a candidate who happens to be female than a man would.

To some extent this is a moot point. Search still remains a male-dominated field, particularly in the largest firms. Korn/Ferry, for instance, has but five female partners out of more than one hundred. If a recruiter calls you from there, chances are it will be a man.

Given the difficulty many women encounter in trying to move up within the larger firms, some women recruiters are starting firms of their own—a trend that leads Allan Stern to say that in the future, the search industry will become a particularly good one for women.

Meanwhile, whether the recruiter who calls you is male or female, it makes no difference. The rules of the game remain the same. For that reason, too, in researching this book, I have not limited myself to women only, but have spoken to both women and men in the executive-search business.

WHY A JOB GOES "OUT TO SEARCH"

To further understand how the search industry works, one should understand why a company hires a search firm to find a candidate:

- The company wants to find someone who is making a mark in his or her field, someone who is happily in place and not a disgruntled, out-of-work executive.
- The available position is at a higher level than is normally served by classified ads.
- Companies don't wish to call employees of competitors directly; executive-search firms act as buffers.
- The company does not have the in-house resources or the

time to fill the position: Finding, screening, and interviewing candidates takes a good deal of time.

- The company has no internal candidates to fill the spot.
- The company wants to see if the external candidates will be better than or equal to its internal candidates.
- The search is highly confidential.
- The job is highly sensitive or highly specialized, or for other reasons is difficult to fill.
- The company has not been able to fill the position itself.
- The company feels that a search firm can do a better job of finding a candidate.
- For internal political reasons, the company wants a "neutral" party—a search firm—to find the candidate.
- If the company is going through a difficult period, or if the circumstances require special explanation, the recruiter can act as a neutral yet well-informed representative of the company.

And so when a recruiter calls you with a possible position, chances are there are some very definite reasons why you're hearing about it from him, rather than reading about it in the classifieds.

CHOOSING THE RIGHT FIRM FOR YOU

And that, in brief, is what a map of the headhunting industry looks like. Why should it matter to you? Because you must also play the matchmaker, identifying those firms and recruiters that are right for you:

- Those that specialize in or have experience in placing people in your industry or function.
- Those that handle positions at the appropriate levels of responsibility.
- Those that handle positions within the appropriate salary range.

- Those that have a reputation for professional, ethical behavior.
- Those that will keep your resume (and your job search) confidential.
- Those that have a reputation for treating people as individuals, not just resumes.

To help you decide:

- When a recruiter calls, ask the following questions:
    - –Are you a retainer or a contingency firm?
    - –Have you worked with this client company before?
    - –Do you specialize in this industry? What is your experience working in this industry?
    - –How long has your firm (or have you) been in business?

- When speaking to a recruiter, make it clear that your conversation—and your resume—are confidential.
- Ask colleagues and friends what their experiences have been with particular recruiters and their firms.
- Find out what people in your trade or professional association have to say about different recruiters. Which ones are good? Which ones are not?

With this information in hand, you are ready for the next step: how to get your head hunted.

3

HOW TO GET YOUR HEAD HUNTED

Now that you understand who is doing the hunting, let us proceed to the question of who is being hunted—and how you can join their ranks.

WHO IS BEING HUNTED?

Big game hunters carefully track their prey through the byways of corporate America. They follow their targets from a distance and then they strike—with a phone call, an opportunity, a sales pitch.

Who are these targets?

"We pick the cream of the crop," says a spokesperson for Russell Reynolds.

"If you're good, we'll identify you," Sydney Reynolds asserts.

The message from these and other exclusive search consultants is clear: Don't call us, we'll call you.

And they will call, eventually: That is, if you are in a position in which you *can* be spotted as a potential target for a call.

But what constitutes a potential target? The preferred profile will depend on the type of firm:

To catch the eye of the largest retainer firms—those that handle the highest-level searches—one should have at least six to ten years of experience and be currently making $60,000 to $75,000 or more.

The smaller retainer firms and specialty retainer firms handling middle- as well as top-level searches are more likely to consider people starting at about the $40,000 to $50,000 level.

Contingency firms specializing in a particular industry or function often handle positions starting at the $20,000 to $30,000 level, up to about the $75,000 to $100,000 range.

Some contingency firms may also work with searches at the $100,000 level and up. Some may handle these higher-level searches on a retainer basis.

Search firms do not handle recent graduates. If you fall into this category, use your college or graduate school placement office instead.

Of course, there are other aspects to the profile as well: Working hard and making a mark in your industry is the first order of business, as always. Ann Powers Kern, a partner at Korn/Ferry, further identifies five areas in which executives might develop their careers:

1. "First, get profit-center responsibility as soon as possible."

2. "Know how to take risks."

3. "Internationalize your career, because so much of today's world is not just the United States."

4. "Learn to communicate effectively. Leaders must also be speakers."

5. "And use mobility, but use it selectively." Companies want to see a breadth of experience, she points out, but "Success is still based on a solid record of sustained achievement."

In tandem with this solid record of achievement, however, one should also develop a public-relations campaign as a way of making yourself a visible player in the industry, Janet Jones-

Parker advises. Or how else will the recruiters know about that solid record of achievement?

In order to understand how to become visible to the recruiters, we must first begin to understand how the hunters approach their hunt.

HOW THE HUNTERS HUNT: FIRST, THEY RESEARCH

The first step in every search is research. To use the lingua franca of the headhunting business, the purpose of research is to "identify the universe"—that is, uncover the names of all the potential candidates for the position in question.

Frequently, particularly in the larger firms, the research and the recruiting functions are divided. The recruiters do the actual recruiting: They talk to client companies, bring in new business, interview potential candidates, and play the go-between as the client and job candidate progress through the rounds of interviews and negotiations.

But it is the researchers who locate and sometimes pre-screen (by means of an initial telephone conversation) the potential job candidates whom the recruiter will then call. The larger firms support substantial research staffs (the great majority of these researchers are women) along with sophisticated computer systems.

At smaller or mid-sized firms unable to afford a full-time research department, Kenneth Cole notes a growing tendency to hire independent researchers on a free-lance basis. These are often researchers who have broken away from the larger firms to form businesses of their own.

At the large firms, researchers tend to be paid less than recruiters and, once typed as a researcher, they often find it difficult to switch to recruiting. Researchers therefore may not appear to be even close to the highest level in a recruiting firm's pecking order, but do not underestimate or forget them. Some break away to form their own independent research or executive-search firms. Some go to other firms as researchers. And still others move to firms that will provide opportunities for them to work as recruiters, not just researchers. So being friendly to a researcher today may yield continuing rewards in the future.

Here's how:

- Researchers feed names to recruiters. If you are in the data bank of an independent researcher working with several firms, your name may turn up for more searches at more firms.
- Today's researcher may be tomorrow's recruiter.
- In the same way that a friendly recruiter will keep you in mind when appropriate openings appear, so will a friendly researcher.

For instance, one executive felt herself highly flattered when a recruiter from a prestigious firm called to court her for a very high-level job opening. Her professional reputation was even stronger than she had thought! And well it might be. But months after her interview with the recruiter took place, she discovered that, in this case at least, her name had been given to the recruiter by none other than an old acquaintance from one of her very first jobs—a woman who was now the head of research for that same prestigious firm.

For these reasons, "It's best to be in the Rolodex of both the researcher and the recruiter," Jeanne Marie Gilbert, a former recruiter and search firm research associate, says. In hunting the headhunter, don't forget the researcher.

Let's visit the researchers' universe now—at least their universe at one of New York's largest and most exclusive recruiting firms.

WELCOME TO THE WONDERFUL WORLD OF RESEARCH

You walk through the wood-paneled waiting area, past the receptionist, and there before you is the research area: It is a maze of cubicles, and within each one a woman sits, scanning directories and periodicals, calling new sources and familiar ones, identifying all the different universes for the different jobs the recruiters seek to fill.

Lining this large rectangular space are solid walls of bookshelves and filing cabinets. The bookshelves are filled with directories bound in red and green and black and brown, paperbacks and hardcovers, small and oversized. Here you will find industry and company directories as well as the directories of professional associations. There are trade journals and conference proceedings. There are heavy reference volumes: *The Directory of Directories* is only one such volume capable of directing you to almost anyone or anything you can possibly think of. The volumes are arranged alphabetically by subject and by industry. Undoubtedly your industry has its place on these shelves, too.

There are alumni magazines from all the Ivy League schools, of course, and the major business schools. And then there are the back issues of the *Wall Street Journal* and the *New York Times*, waiting to be read and clipped for whatever information they contain.

You circle around the room until you are back where you began, and then you notice an entrance to another complex— the computer room. Here, at the computer keyboard, you may punch in the particular characteristics you seek in a potential candidate—the number of years of experience in this field, combined with a background in that function—and out spew the names. Want to get more specific? List the size of the company in which the ideal candidate will have gained that experience, or punch in a graduate degree, or perhaps limit the search to a single geographic area. You'll get a list of those names, too.

Of course, there are any number of filing cabinets in this room; there are always more files. On another floor you'll find the archives—the files of searches too old now to shed much light on new searches even in the same area.

As you gaze at the books, the files, and the computers, you wonder at the thoroughness with which these researchers carry out their jobs, finding names and identifying each new universe for each new job search. These are expert detectives at work, after all. They know where to look for their clues, their sources, and their likely suspects.

And yet you're still a little puzzled. Why haven't they called you? Why wasn't your name produced by the computer?

The answer is elementary, the researchers tell you. In order for us to identify you as being a part of our universe, you've got to appear in it! How can we possibly know we should call you, they will rightly point out, if you're not in the directories, the periodicals, the newspapers, the computer files, the paper files? Make yourself visible to us, they say, and we just might become visible to you. Because listen: However good you are, how can we call you if, according to our research, you don't even exist?

A FEW WORDS ON RESEARCH TECHNIQUES

How do researchers get all that information, anyway? At the firm we have just visited, research is conducted in a highly professional manner: First the researchers turn to whatever public information is available. They buy whatever directories are available in the industries they cover. They subscribe to and read the professional journals. They clip articles appearing in the business and general press. They consult data bases. They consult their own data base.

Then they talk to people in the industries they're being paid to track. Friendly sources help them identify potential candidates whose names they have not found. Sometimes particularly helpful sources will provide them with other professional directories that the researchers cannot obtain themselves. These sources cooperate willingly, knowing the purpose to which the information will be put, trusting it will be used confidentially.

If, after all of this, the researchers need still more information or more names for the particular search in which they're engaged, they may also call a company likely to employ potential candidates and say, "I'm addressing correspondence; could you give me the name and exact spelling of the vice-president of public relations?" When asked who they are, the researchers may reply, "I'm a consultant." If the secretary requests a further explanation, these researchers may prefer to hang up.

Now wait a second, you say: Aren't we stepping into a twilight area of what is an acceptable method of obtaining information and what is not?

While one former researcher finds this particular practice "relatively benign," she points to other strategies for obtaining information that are clearly unethical—primarily the "funny phone call" technique by which a researcher attempts to get information about people working in a company by misrepresenting who she is and why she is calling.

"You can call and pretend you're in another office and that your directory is outdated," the former researcher says. "You can call and say you're the president's secretary calling to find out something. Or you can call and misrepresent yourself as a reporter or a graduate student doing a report and who needs information. There are many sleazy ways."

And there's the "classic" phone call, she says, which goes this way: "You call the secretary and say, 'I was at a restaurant last night, and I overheard a conversation of the guy sitting at the next table who happened to mention he works for your company. He left this whole run of computer stuff on the chair next to him, and I'd like to get it back to him. I don't know his name, but he's about medium height or taller with dark hair, and I'm sure I'd know his name if I heard it! Could you help me find him?' And then, of course, the secretary tries to be helpful and you get the name and title of everyone in the department."

In another questionable tactic, a researcher will call, saying she is recruiting for a fictitious position. In reality, she is trying to get biographical information about people in the company.

Why do some otherwise professional researchers resort to these tactics? "There can be tremendous pressure" to get the names, phone numbers, and biographical information about potential candidates, the former researcher explains. "The recruiter says, 'Get that information, and I don't care how. I don't want to know.' And that translates into this other kind of behavior."

"My professionalism and my integrity are more important to me than doing these things," the researcher concludes. "But for some researchers, the pressure is there."

Although reputable search firms and researchers do not engage in these practices, if you do get a "funny phone call," be on guard against unwittingly giving out confidential information about yourself or your colleagues that you would not wish to share.

VISIBLE TARGETS, INVISIBLE EXECUTIVES

Let's assume that highly reputable researchers and recruiters are conducting a search in your area of expertise. Perhaps you would be a good candidate for the position. Perhaps you would like to be considered for it. Will the firm be able to find you?

If your name appears in any of the directories or other print sources the researchers regularly consult—or if you are mentioned by any of the industry sources whom they call—the answer is yes. If you have become visible in the directories, or visible to people in your industry, you are also visible to the recruiters.

But if you have not found your way into the directories, if people in the industry do not know your name, then, as far as the recruiter is concerned, you are invisible.

The message is clear: To the visible belong the phone calls. Invisible loners beware.

"Being visible comes way before getting into the computers," says Marge Baxter, an associate at Handy Associates and a career counselor.

Baxter confirms that it is not simply through doing a good job that people find their way into the search firm's files—although that solid record certainly is the basic foundation on which to build any career. Beyond that, however, the key is— you guessed it—visibility. "You want to be known to the people the headhunters call, until you yourself become one of those people that the headhunters call," Baxter comments.

Here's why:

- Because it's magical thinking to assume that just because you do a good job, everyone will beat a path to your door. First, they have to know that your door exists.
- Because if you find yourself out of a job as a result of a takeover or a corporate reorganization, you certainly want your name to be mentioned to recruiters or potential employers.
- Because, even though you may be perfectly happy at the moment, it certainly can't hurt to be thought of when an attractive position becomes available.

There are several practical steps you can take to raise your visibility profile. The first step starts with that much abused word—networking.

A FEW WORDS ABOUT THAT MUCH ABUSED WORD: NETWORKING

Networking: How overused, abused, and misused that word has become. And yet we all exist within a community—a network, if you will—of mutually supportive colleagues, associates, friends, and acquaintances. A network that is mutually supportive: that is the key phrase, I think—and the one that is most often ignored.

For if you think of a network in that way, rather than as a means of individuals selfishly using each other, you also see that:

- Networking is not a means of collecting business cards, a way to maneuver a cursory handshake and hello at a cocktail party into a business contact.
- Networking does not mean taking the narrowly careerist view as you go through life, rating everyone in your Rolodex by how much he or she can help you professionally.

A network, in short, means give *and* take—not just take, take, take:

- Networking means giving favors, not just asking for them.
- Networking means helping others, passing along to other newcomers what someone once passed along to you.
- Networking means trading favors, not just asking for them.
- Networking is for people who take the long view in their careers. After all, "what goes around, comes around."
- Networking, ultimately, is based on mutual interests; in the long run, the cold-blooded user has no credibility.

How does one define a network? A professional network might include, first, the people with whom you work at your company—your peers, superiors, and subordinates. Outside your company, there are other friends and professional acquaintances—colleagues from former jobs, people with whom you formerly worked at your current company, and members of the various professional associations to which you belong.

Then there is the more personal network outside of work, at whose core lie your family and friends. In addition, perhaps you perform volunteer work for a community charity, sing in a choral group, have become active in the neighborhood association, sit on a not-for-profit board, or simply take part in an informal women's dinner group. The acquaintances and friends formed in these activities also constitute a network.

Calling upon the individuals in these different networks as you would have them call upon you—not to "use" you, but as part of a mutual support system—may be an idealistic view of what networking means. But in the end, I believe, this is the only attitude that works.

YOUR NETWORK OF VISIBILITY

"The recruiter just called me straight out of the blue," one executive says. "It was a fluke—the recruiter was given my name by a friend of mine," another one asserts. "It was sheer luck that the recruiter called," a third reports.

But it's neither luck nor a fluke: on further questioning it turns out that these executives had all become "visible" to the recruiters in one way or another, either through trade associations or through word-of-mouth—in short, through networking.

The more extensive your network is, the more visible you become to more people. The more varied your network is, the more visible you become, not only within the industry but within other circles as well. And because the world is small, these circles often have a way of overlapping: Your friend in the chorus may know someone who also works in your industry, who just happens to be looking for someone to fill a position; or she knows a recruiter who might be interested in knowing you. Or your friend from the trade association might be (and probably is) a source to whom a number of recruiters turn.

In sum, doing an excellent job is the bedrock upon which careers are based. Now let's get the word out about just how good you are.

Becoming Visible Within Your Organization

First of all, Baxter says, become visible to the people within your organization. Of course, if you spent your time *only* doing that, you would have no time to do the job itself. But do think about trying at least one or two of the following suggestions:

- Volunteer to participate on an inter-departmental task force or *ad hoc* committee.
- Send information to or write something for the company newsletter. (Warning: If you write about something your department accomplished, don't make yourself sound like a hot dog; always give credit to staff members and colleagues.) Be a friendly and helpful source to the newsletter editor.
- Attend company conferences. You'll have an unusual opportunity to hobnob with other executives from your company to whom you might not ordinarily have access.
- Join the company softball team or fitness program. You'll get to know colleagues in an informal setting.
- Offer to work with the personnel department on a lunch hour "enrichment" program—whether it's a workout program or a series of brown-bag luncheon talks. Volunteer to give one of the first talks.
- Make yourself known to the people in the public-relations department. Let them know that when reporters call for stories and need information, you'll be helpful.

Becoming Visible Outside the Organization

Next come some tips on how to become visible to people *outside* your particular company:

Hire consultants. When you work on projects with outside vendors or consultants, get to know both them and their firms. You never know when consultants whom you've favorably impressed will want to recruit you themselves—or will think to pass on your name to an executive recruiter.

Encourage your company to send you to business conferences or training programs. You'll not only spend a week to your immediate professional advantage, you'll also have the opportunity to meet, in relatively relaxed circumstances, an interesting cross section of executives from other industries and other parts of the country.

Join professional associations. You'll meet colleagues who share your professional interests and from whom you can gain a broader perspective of what's going on in your industry. Executive recruiters who specialize in a particular area sometimes join these associations. Even if they are not allowed to join, they often turn to association members as sources and to the association directory for names.

There may be several associations open to you. Some recruiters suggest joining several. Others advise you to find out which ones in your profession, industry, or area of specialty are the most highly respected and then concentrate on those. The main point is to join—and then to become active.

Are the membership fees a little stiff? Remember that you're paying to have your name in a directory—to be a part of the headhunters' universe.

Should you join a women's professional group? Yes, but it should not be the only group you join. Some women's groups —the Financial Women's Association of New York, for instance—have excellent reputations, not only in the industry but among executive recruiters as well. But, depending on the group, recruiters may prefer to look at co-ed directories. Why not join both groups?

After you've joined and gotten your name in the directory, don't be shy. Be active in the organization: Join a committee, help organize an event, volunteer to speak at a meeting or conference. Speak up and show your expertise. If possible, get your name in the conference brochure. Why? Because researchers collect conference brochures. The speech titles and panel topics tell them what the pertinent issues are in the industry and, more important, who knows a lot about them.

Take part in professional conferences. Even if you don't give a speech, become involved in some aspect of planning the conference. Recruiters often call conference coordinators as industry sources. If you helped plan the conference, the coordinator will know your name.

Volunteer your services. Put your interest in or enthusiasm for a hobby or charity to good use. Become involved with a non-profit organization—whether it's the Sierra Club or the Choral Society, the Junior League or the local Coalition for the Homeless. Volunteer, become active, and work for a worthy cause. Do pro bono work, help organize a benefit, join a non-profit board. In addition to doing something worthwhile, you will expand your circle of acquaintance and have an opportunity to sharpen, expand, refine, or discover skills you may not have had a chance to develop at work. Your good deeds may yield good personal publicity in both the nonprofit organization and in your office.

Send your news to alumni publications. The alumni notes section of your college magazine provides an excellent opportunity to let people know what you are doing. It is free publicity, targeted at an audience that is interested in knowing what you are doing—your old school network. Headhunters tend to read the undergraduate and graduate bulletins of the upper-echelon schools. Women who went to all-women's schools, however, beware: While recruiters will religiously read the alumni bulletins from Harvard or Columbia, most headhunters won't necessarily see the *Radcliffe Quarterly* or the *Barnard News* unless the recruiter happens to be female, an alumna herself, or a male married to an alumna. Therefore, write your news to both the male and female counterparts of your schools (*Harvard Magazine* as well as the *Radcliffe Quarterly*, for instance). And if you're married, have your husband write in his news—along with yours.

Write an article. Do you have a particular specialty or area of interest? Write an article based on your expertise. Writing for an industry publication will introduce you to several audiences: professional colleagues and associates, search firms and others interested in tracking your field, and the editors of the magazine itself. A tip: The editor of the industry journal is often one of the first people a recruiter or researcher starting a search will call to find out who's who, who's doing what, and who's hot.

Write another article. Is there an angle or slant to your industry journal article that would interest a more general audience? Take a broader view of your subject and write an article for the local newspaper, an alumni magazine, a general-interest magazine, or a national publication like the *New York Times* or *Wall Street Journal.* Recruiters clip these articles for their files. Make sure the bio-line tells enough about you so they can find you!

Get quoted in the press. Simply by having published these articles, you will have established yourself as an expert. As a result, reporters or others following the industry will begin to call you as an expert source, as someone to quote in *their* articles. Be friendly and helpful, and you may well become someone who is quoted frequently. Recruiters will get to know your name, too.

Attend alumni reunions, professional conventions, and other similar occasions. They provide the one day a year you have to meet or keep in touch with friends and colleagues from around the country.

Become active in your alumni association. If you're not interested in the scholarship committee or interviewing prospective undergraduates, volunteer to give a talk or be part of a panel on career opportunities in your profession. You'll not only meet bright young graduates who might be good resources for your organization, you will have the chance to get to know or work with people in the college placement office— people who are constantly coming into contact with recruiters from many companies as well as others who have achieved certain levels of recognition in their fields. You also may find yourself on a panel with an internal recruiter from a company in which you're interested.

Join a search committee. You may have the chance to join a search committee as part of your job or as a result of your involvement with alumni associations or nonprofit organizations. In either case, you will more than likely have the opportunity to review a variety of search firms vying for the search, and in the process you will also have the chance to meet a number of recruiters.

Stay in touch with people. Don't let people forget you. Isn't that why we invented the custom of sending Christmas cards?

NEXT STEP: TARGETING YOUR PREY

Another way to become visible is to contact the search firms yourself. But with so many firms in existence, how do you choose the firms that are most likely to have the best opportunities for you? To answer this question, you must research the search firms in the same way that they would research you.

First, gather the names:

Talk to people in your professional associations. Whom do they recommend? With whom have they had experiences? What were their experiences like, in general? Do any recruiters belong to the associations you belong to? Have any given talks or participated on panel discussions? What kind of an impression did they make?

The next time you have to hire someone, ask your colleagues about the different recruiters they've used—purely as background for potentially hiring someone, of course!

Even if you are not hiring someone, ask colleagues about their experiences with recruiters. (Ask discreetly. You don't want to sound as if you're about to mail a million resumes tomorrow.) If your friends have hired recruiters, what were their impressions of the firms they reviewed? Why did they hire one recruiter but reject another? Similarly, if they were interviewed by recruiters as potential candidates, what were their experiences?

Be attentive to office shoptalk about headhunters. Say, for

instance, you hear that a mutual acquaintance is switching jobs. It's not at all unnatural to ask, *Oh, by the way, did she use a recruiter? I wonder how she got hooked up with that firm? Gee, have you had experiences with headhunters yourself? By the way, which ones have you heard are good?*

Make friends with people in the human resources department. They can give you names of people they've worked with or have heard are good. They can also alert you to which firms the company has hired recently—ones to whom you should therefore *not* send your resume.

If you're out of a job, ask your outplacement counselor about firms that have been particularly receptive to people in a situation similar to yours.

Read your trade publications. Which recruiters are quoted frequently? Which firms advertise in your industry publications? What do your colleagues say about those firms?

File the answers in your head—or better yet, in an actual file for future reference.

For more names, check the listings at the back of this book and the other resources listed.

Now that you have the names, screen them further. Go through a preliminary checklist to discover the following about each firm in your possible universe.

Does the firm:

    ___ *Specialize in your industry*

    ___ *Handle your job function within a variety of industries*

    ___ *Handle your job level and higher*

    ___ *Handle your salary range*

Is the firm:

    ___ *Contingency firm*

    ___ *Retainer firm*

    ___ *Based locally*

    ___ *(Inter)National firm with nearby local office*

You know about the firm because:

_____ *You know people who have had good experiences with them*

_____ *You hear it has a good reputation, but don't know anyone who has worked with them.*

_____ *So-so reputation or worse*

_____ *No knowledge of the firm's reputation*

_____ *Your company has hired them within the last two years*

_____ *Your division or department has hired them within the last two years*

You'll find some of these answers by talking to colleagues and associates. For more information, call the firm, explain that you plan to write to them, and ask the questions directly. For instance:

Are you a retainer or contingency firm? Do you handle searches in the advertising area? All aspects of advertising, or primarily the creative end? In what salary range and at what levels of responsibility? And who in the firm specializes in [name your] area? Would it be possible to send me a corporate brochure?

Research the firms that you wish to contact as carefully as their research departments would screen you. The better the match, the better chance you'll have of hearing from a recruiter.

CONTACTING THE HEADHUNTER

Now that you have identified the firms you're particularly interested in, you are ready for the next step: making contact with the recruiter. How do you go about doing that?

Have a friend or colleague call a recruiter on your behalf. The best person to call is someone who has *hired* the recruiter —who has buttered the recruiter's bread and to whom a favor is owed. The next best person is someone whom the recruiter has placed in a job or who has been a good source for the recruiter in the past.

Once your friend makes the call, what then? It depends on the recruiter. Some recruiters will prefer for you to follow up by calling them; others will call you. The recruiter may or may not ask to meet you in person, may or may not ask to see a resume. (If the recruiter does ask for a resume, give it to him only with the understanding that it is to be kept confidential.)

If the recruiter does meet you, it will probably be for no more than half an hour as part of a "courtesy" interview, so-called because it is a courtesy to you and a favor to the mutual friend. After all, chances are that no appropriate search is in the offing. Then why are you meeting? We've already established that the recruiter is performing a favor; if the person he meets happens to be appropriate for a current or future search, that's a bonus.

Your purpose in meeting the recruiter is not to sell yourself for a particular job (there probably is none), but to present yourself as both a potential candidate for future searches and as a possible source. Let the recruiter know that he may call you to ask for suggestions about other possible candidates; if you're able to do favors for him now, perhaps he'll be able to do something for you in the future. (For more on this, see Chapter 4, page 126.)

Before asking your friend to make the call for you, however, make certain that the recruiter handles searches in your area. Don't waste your friend's, the recruiter's, or your own time.

Should you "cold call" a recruiting firm? Logic would seem to say that if the recruiters can cold call *you*, why can't you cold call *them*? Because a cold call to a recruiter may yield nothing more than a cold shoulder.

If you have no mutual acquaintance or other referral, call cold only if you have the specific name of a person within the firm—along with a specific reason for calling. Simply asking, "I'm wondering if you would be interested in seeing my resume?" isn't likely to grab anyone's attention. A brief description of your work history—depending on what that work history consists of and how well it matches the kinds of searches the firm is currently working on—might elicit a bit more interest. Breaking the ice by saying, "I heard you speak at the Widgets Professional Association last week," may earn you a few minutes more on the telephone. Mentioning a mutual alumni tie or the name of some other mutual acquaintance might be enough to secure a brief courtesy meeting.

Let's say you work in Cleveland. A business trip takes you to New York City, home of more executive-search firms than any city on earth, including one or two firms to whose recruiters you'd like to make yourself known. You decide to call at least one firm, identify yourself, describe who you are, and see if someone in the firm might want to meet with you. One executive found everyone he called more than willing to meet with him after they heard his story, which began this way: "Hello, I am visiting from Frankfurt, West Germany, and I am only in town for today. Do you think it would be possible for me to speak to somebody?" Of course, if you use this technique, you'd better be telling the truth!

Should you send a resume cold? Only send your resume cold after you have screened and researched the firms carefully. Why waste postage mailing material to recruiters that have never handled a search in your industry?

If you are currently employed, make sure your need for confidentiality will be respected. If you're writing to contingency firms, Janet Jones-Parker advises telling the recruiter that you will go on interviews *only* if the recruiter has asked and received your permission to send your resume to a company for a given job. Such conditions are not only difficult to outline in a letter designed to introduce you to your best advantage, however; if you don't trust the firm to respect your confidentiality to begin with, why are you writing?

If you are actively looking anyway, if your boss knows you're looking, or if you are in outplacement, then sending a resume cold obviously carries far less risk. What do you have to lose if your boss happens to hear that you're looking, if he knows it already?

*At what point in your career should you think about con-
tacting headhunters?* It depends on the headhunter you wish
to contact: Is it a firm handling lower- and middle-level positions or one handling higher-level positions?

"At some point as a professional—and it should be sometime after three years or so—you should start to know who the
players are, who can do something for you if and when the
time comes, and that group has to include headhunters," comments Howard Stevens, whose firm, the Bankers Register, fills
many mid-range positions.

Recruiters whose searches tend to be at a slightly higher
level suggest that job seekers begin to make contact with recruiting firms only at the point at which they have crossed the
line from being an entry-level executive to a mid-level position
or higher, usually five to seven years into a career.

Both contingency and retainer recruiters agree that executives who are still new to their careers should *not* send their
resumes to recruiters. If you're just moving up from entry-level
positions, you're probably at too low a level to earn serious
attention, and your efforts will be wasted. "I don't think a two-
to-three-year person should be going to an executive recruiter
with expectations that they're going to be able to help you get a
job," says Sydney Reynolds. And from most recruiters' point
of view, you will be considered entry level until you have at
least five years of experience.

To how many recruiters should you send your resume? The
answer depends on your current job status. If you only wish to
test the water, be selective. You want to see what's available
without jeopardizing your confidentiality or your current position. Write to no more than a handful, just to get your name
in the data base.

But if you find yourself out of a job or if you are in outplacement, you have nothing to lose by sending your resume to as
many recruiters as you deem appropriate. "It's a one-shot
deal," Howard Williams points out. Why not try to target as
many places as possible? However, since recruiters often tend
to be wary of executives who are not currently employed, ask

your outplacement counselor if he or she can recommend recruiters who have been receptive to people in your situation.

If you are actively seeking a new job, but your current job is
not in jeopardy, be selective. You want to get your resume out
without papering the industry with it. You don't want several
competing contingency firms to send your resume to the same
company—or, by accident, to your boss's golfing buddy. Mini-
mize the risk by setting up a meeting with the recruiter and
establishing the ground rules—to whom he can send your resume and when—*before* you give it to him.

How worried should you be about confidentiality? "We do
our utmost so that no one knows that we're talking, except the
candidate and myself," Ann Powers Kern says. "If I'm working
on a search with a search committee, I always warn them
about confidentiality and tell them not even to share information with their spouses."

All reputable recruiters feel the same way. However, there
are times when information may slip out inadvertently: for example, when a contingency firm markets a candidate too
widely, or when a firm, in checking a candidate's references,
accidentally spills the beans. So how do you balance your
need to look with your concern for privacy?

"There is always that element of risk when you're looking
for a job and you are currently employed, that somebody will
get overly zealous and will contact somebody in your company," Janet Jones-Parker comments, "but it doesn't happen
very often, and you have to be willing to take the risk."

Further, she says, "A person who is actively interviewing
probably either has already or will very shortly come to the
conclusion that they're going to leave anyway. So if someone
found out and you had to leave, then you are ending up in the
same place. By the very nature of your interviewing, you've
made the decision to leave. And so it's not as much of a risk as
people think."

The more carefully you screen the firms you contact, the
lower your risk will be.

WRITING A RESUME THAT WON'T GET THROWN AWAY

Executive-recruiting firms receive thousands of resumes each year from thousands of successful executives. The more exclusive and well known the firm is, the more resumes it receives. The numbers can run upwards of twenty thousand a year for some firms. They can't possibly help each person who writes to them. In fact, some recruiters estimate that the chances of matching an unsolicited resume with a search they happen to be working on at the moment is well below 5 percent. And even if someone in the firm does read your resume—and most firms say that they will read resumes that come in over the transom—how do you write a resume that will go into a computer file rather than the circular file?

Getting the researchers to simply look at your resume is the first step, but you'd better grab their attention fast. "We get about 2,000 resumes per month," says Marge Baxter of Handy Associates. "Mondays are the heaviest—they come in mailbags."

And although someone besides a secretary does read the resumes, "at least 90 to 95 percent of them get thrown away," Baxter admits. Why? "It's not that these are bad resumes; they're just inappropriate."

Baxter lists the main reasons for being inappropriate as follows:

- The firm doesn't handle the industry or function of the resume-sender.
- The resume-sender has not reached a high-enough level in salary or responsibility to be considered by this particular firm.
- The resume-sender does not convey (or does not know) the kinds of opportunities for which he or she would like to be considered.

If you don't want your resume thrown away at the start, do your research. Know to whom you're sending your resume, what you want your resume to convey, and what you want to do next.

FOUR COMMON RESUME MISTAKES

The thought of writing a resume can be daunting, but a resume is nothing more or less than a marketing tool, Baxter points out. Its purpose is simple: to get you noticed and to get your foot in the door.

Whom do you want to notice you? If you've done your research, you'll know not to waste time knocking on the door of a search firm or company that would have no place to use your talents, however talented you are.

Now that you've targeted the appropriate firms, you're ready to knock on their doors and send them your resume. But in writing your resume, beware of what Baxter terms the four most frequent resume mistakes—errors she calls "sins of commission *and* omission."

Mistake Number One: The resume writer fails to give any sense of the company for which she is working. Never assume that everyone in the world is familiar with your company. "Let's say you give me a resume that says the MCT Corporation, Greenwich, Connecticut," says Jeanne Marie Gilbert. "Well, I don't know what that is! And so I throw it away. Because it means nothing to me and I have no time for this."

Always include a line or two in your resume—or in your cover letter—describing the company or the specific division of the company for which you work. Instead of writing, "Pratt Whitney," write: "Pratt Whitney, an x-million-dollar division of United Technologies, a Fortune 20 company."

Mistake Number Two: The resume writer fails to include any departmental or reporting structure. Always place your job within the context of your organization as a whole.

"A resume that says, 'Reports to senior vice-president, operations, supervises 410'—that gets thrown out," Baxter comments. "Because you don't supervise 410 people. You supervise them through seventeen people who are directly reporting to you. You have to give a scope of the structure and your place in it."

"Or say that you're a tax analyst," Baxter continues. What the researcher will want to know is the following: "How many other people are tax analysts? Who does what? How is the job divided—geographically, by product line, by subsidiary, by type of project, or what? Are you a senior tax analyst? What is the context?"

The following description would answer all these questions: "Senior-most of six analysts, domestic products, reporting to vice-president, taxes."

Note that in listing the people to whom you report, it's the people's positions that the recruiter wants, not the specific names. The researcher/recruiter is interested in the way your job is structured. Unless you work for Lee Iacocca, chances are the superior's name won't mean much. But if you do name drop, make sure, first, that it's a name worth dropping, and second, that you really do report directly to that person.

Mistake Number Three: The resume writer omits the dates of her education. "This is a tip-off to companies, personnel people, and search firms that you're hiding something," Baxter says. It suggests that you don't wish to reveal your age or there is a gap in your working record. "It raises a question that is needlessly raised." Such information tends to come out in an interview, anyway, Baxter points out. So why raise a question at the start?

Mistake Number Four: The resume writer adapts her job description from the company's internal job description. The job descriptions written by personnel departments "are some of the worst-written documents in the corporate world," Baxter says. Beware, therefore, of transforming a badly written corporate document into a badly written resume. Just think about it: If you can barely understand the personnel department's clotted language, how can you expect a stranger to interpret it in the thirty seconds it takes to decide whether to save a resume or throw it out? It's far better to use your own wording and be concise.

More Resume Don'ts

Those may be the most common errors, Baxter says, but there are many others that crop up more often than she would like, and her list of Resume-Writing Don'ts is a lengthy one:

Don't lead with irrelevant information. Instead, lead with the most relevant and important "news" about yourself: your most impressive position to date, along with your responsibilities and achievements in that role.

But what if the most impressive job you've had is not your current position? There are two options. If you are using a functional resume—which organizes your experience by types of experience rather than by strict chronology—then you would automatically put this information at the top of the list, anyway.

However, if you are writing a chronological resume—which is the kind of resume that most recruiters prefer—you can highlight a specific job in a brief "objectives" section at the top of the resume, in your cover letter, or both. In the resume's chronological job listing, you can accent a particular position further by the amount of space given or the wording used.

Remember: The recruiter will have decided whether or not to keep your resume in the time it takes to read the first half or two-thirds of the first page. Who has time to plod through detailed descriptions of a first job that has nothing to do with what you're doing now? If you begin your resume that way, the person reading it will get no further—and your resume won't get any further, either.

Instead, take a lesson from newspaper reporting: The lead paragraph in a news story always contains the most important facts; read that and you have the gist of the story. Each paragraph that follows contains the other facts in their descending order of importance, with the least relevant parts appearing last.

Don't squeeze your resume onto one page if it doesn't fit on one page. In college, we were taught that a resume should never exceed one page. And it's true that when you're starting your career, you may not have done enough to fill even that single page. But once you've achieved a certain level in your career, one—or even two—pages simply may not be enough. At that point, the one-page rule should be ignored.

In fact, job seekers who reduce the type size on their resumes in order to fit everything onto a single page may be doing themselves more harm than good. After all, why make the resume difficult to read by putting everything into fine print—particularly when you're trying to headline your achievements? A far better way to reduce the size of your resume is to be selective in the information you include. For instance, do you need to go into detail about that summer job you had in college?

Don't be wordy. The fewer words the better. "Half the words can be cut out of some resumes," Baxter observes. Some wording tips: Start each paragraph with verbs, preferably those that begin with consonants; they sound stronger. Instead of saying initiated or established, therefore, say performed, participated, created, developed, designed, managed, and supervised.

Don't use a functional resume. These were all the rage some years back—the kind of resume that, instead of presenting your career chronologically, organized your experience according to different skills and projects. For people wishing to switch careers, or for those still in entry-level positions, a functional resume can be very useful, career counselors advise, because it can highlight certain aspects of a career that might otherwise get lost in a more conventional presentation.

But the most frustrating thing about these resumes is that they tend to be fuzzy when it comes to providing exact information about where you have worked, exactly in what capacity, and when.

And that is why executive recruiters do not like them.

"People *hate* functional resumes," Jeanne Marie Gilbert emphasizes. "It won't tell you what you need to know—what the person's done, where he's been, what are the dates."

In choosing a format, organize the resume in a way that makes sense for you. "People tend to see formats other people have used and force-fit their own resumes into that," Marge Baxter comments. "This often doesn't work. My advice is to just write on sheets of paper everything you'd like to get in, and then see the format that emerges."

Don't include your college grade-point average or SAT scores. This might have been helpful information when you were applying for your first job, but at this stage in your career, who cares? One would hope that you have other, more recent achievements to list instead.

Don't include your high-school alma mater. It's one thing if you went to a prestigious prep school (particularly if you happen to know that the person to whom you are sending your resume is also an alumna or alumnus). But as a general rule, the fact that you went to Metropolitan High School in Big City, USA won't impress too many people. There are a few exceptions, however. You *may* use this to your advantage, for instance, if you want to emphasize the fact that, although you went to an Ivy League college and graduate school, you were not a preppy, but a self-made woman from the public school system.

Don't get carried away in the personal section. The personal section at the end of the resume may be optional, but most people choose to include some humanizing information about themselves. But how human is too human? Or not human enough? Distinctive achievements in community or nonprofit organizations definitely should appear—the fact, for instance, that you are a member of a nonprofit board, or chairman of the benefit committee for a charity.

More personal accomplishments can also appear, but only *if* they really are distinctive accomplishments. "The fact that you may be a jogger is absolutely irrelevant—everyone's a jogger," Baxter points out, "but the fact that you completed the last four New York City Marathons should go in."

Be selective; what you consider to be an achievement someone else may not. Don't include your husband's golf handicap or other inappropriate details, for instance. Baxter reports reading a resume that, in fact, did include both the executive's and his wife's golf handicap. "I have no idea why he did include it," she says, "but I do know that they play a lot of golf!" The information may have grabbed her attention, but hardly for the best reason.

Ask yourself how you want to come across and what tone you want to set. For instance, activities like riding or sailing can sound snobbish, Baxter warns. For some companies that might be absolutely the right tone to set, but for others it might be an immediate turnoff.

Finally, remember that the personal section is not true confessions, Baxter emphasizes. There is no need to include your maiden name, your husband's profession, or the ages of your children. If the recruiter is interested in uncovering these facts, he will.

Never write, "Resume of" at the top of your resume. What else is it?

And don't ever, ever lie on a resume. "We uncover things more frequently than we would like," says Ann Powers Kern, a partner at Korn/Ferry. Resume "inflaters" are not related to age, sex, or job experience, she says. "People who do this sort of thing often perceive it the same way they do cheating the Internal Revenue Service: They don't consider it immoral. But we see it in a different light." The personnel director of a Fortune 500 Company states it more bluntly: "People who lie on resumes simply won't be hired. If they lie there, they may lie about other things, too." Some people may consider it pure gamesmanship to inflate certain accomplishments on a resume—making it sound as if they were the only brains behind a successful new marketing program, rather than just one of four people on the project team—but those in a position to hire will see such behavior differently: as a display of questionable judgment and shady ethical standards. So remember what Mark Twain said: "When in doubt, tell the truth. It will confound your enemies and astound your friends."

A SAMPLE RESUME

The following sample resume is a straightforward, concise summary that presents the executive's experience and education:

Jill M. Jones
123 Fourth Street
Cleveland, Ohio
(216) 999-9999

GENERAL LIGHTING COMPANY, Cleveland, Ohio.
A $2 billion diversified electrical and electronics firm.

Special Project Manager, Strategic Planning, Product Development Division of the Lighting Business Group ($250 million), 1985—Present. Report directly to Senior Vice-President, Product Development Division. Manage staff of ten assistant managers, analysts, and planners.

Headed team that developed and implemented marketing plan that led New Idea Bulbs to regain market dominance. Key strategy elements included repositioning the product as well as a reorganizing of the distribution system, in view of changing consumer needs. Concurrently worked on developing an improved manufacturing process to achieve a competitive cost advantage. Improved from $10 million loss in 1984 to $5 million gain in 1986.

Group Product Manager, New Light Bulbs, 1983-1985.
Responsible for two light bulb lines ($150 million). Supervised three product managers. Reported to Assistant Vice-President, Product Development.

Directed marketing campaign that successfully repositioned previously unprofitable New Light Bulbs line, increasing sales 23 percent in first year.

Senior Product Manager, Novelty Bulbs ($75 million), 1981-1983. Reported to Group Product Manager, Novelty Bulbs.

Helped develop marketing plan that introduced the new

Novelty Bulbs line, gaining a 3.5 market share in first two years. This performance garnered a commitment to expand production 25 percent and fund reserach for other new products. Won Company Manager of the Year Award, 1982.

ABC ADVERTISING, CHICAGO, ILLINOIS (Third largest advertising agency in Chicago)
    Rose from Account Supervisor to Assistant Vice-President for marketing, 1975-1979. Responsible for account supervision and developing product marketing plans to increase market share. Major accounts included Colgate, Brim, and Virginia Slims.

EDUCATION

| The Wharton School | University of Pennsylvania |
| M.B.A.—Marketing, May 1981 | Philadelphia, Pennsylvania |

Pennsylvania State University	University Park, Pennsylvania
BA—History Major, May 1975	
Summa cum laude	

PERSONAL

Vice-President, Ohio League of Women Voters;
Board of Directors, National Marketing Trade association

NOW THAT YOUR RESUME IS READY...
A FEW WORDS ABOUT COVER LETTERS

Cover letters are written to highlight or emphasize some salient fact about you and your background. Although a bland or uninformative cover letter ("Enclosed please find my resume...") won't get your resume thrown away, a good one *can* help your cause by summarizing who you are or by giving a particular slant or headline on what you've achieved. A good cover letter, therefore, should do the following:

• Succinctly tell the recruiter who you are.
• Tell the recruiter exactly what you *want*.

Cover letters, like resumes, should be concise and straightforward. Similarly, they should avoid trite or overused words as well as buzz words and jargon. As always, be precise, specific, and concrete.

This advice might sound obvious, until you start to read some of the cover letters that recruiters receive. Here are some actual examples, followed by comments, in parentheses, from Marge Baxter:

- "I recently learned that your firm is quite active in recruiting upper-level executives for management positions." (Well, that's nice, but is that the only thing you know about our firm? Why are you writing us in particular?)
- "I am creative and energetic, with the skills to handle bottom-line responsibility.... My credentials are impeccable." (The letter-writer indicates nothing about what she does or does not want, though she does manage to include a number of trite phrases.)
- "My objective is to secure a position where I can use my broad experience and contribute in a manner that makes a difference." (That certainly *sounds* good, but what, exactly, does that objective *mean*? Make what kind of difference, how, and in what way?)

Rather than send both a resume and a cover letter, some people prefer to incorporate the resume within the cover letter, to form what is called a broadcast letter. It is nothing more than a resume written in narrative form. Some career counselors, including Nella Barkley of the John Crystal Center, recommend this method. Done well, it can effectively place your career experience within the broader context of your career goals.

However, it is often harder for people to write a full-length narrative letter/resume than it is to compose the sharp phrases of a resume, Baxter comments. Use the form that works best for you.

A SAMPLE COVER LETTER

Dear Mr. Recruiter:

Over the last decade, I have taken on marketing and
management assignments of increasing responsibility at
General Lighting Company, a $2 billion diversified
electrical and electronics company, and, prior to that, at
A/B Advertising of Chicago.

My achievements include leading the management
team responsible for repositioning two declining light
bulb brands, directing the development and
implementation of successful marketing plans for new
products, and working with management teams that
successfully increased the sales and distribution of
several established brands.

I am particularly interested in small, growth-oriented
companies or consulting groups where my experience as
a strategic and marketing analyst can be used to fullest
advantage.

I have enclosed my resume and would be pleased to
answer any questions you may have. Please feel free to
contact me at my office or at home.

Sincerely,

Jill M. Jones

FOLLOWING UP 101:
TO CALL OR NOT TO CALL...

Because the large volume of resumes most firms receive pre-
cludes their sending any acknowledgment, don't be surprised
if your letter is greeted with complete silence, regardless of

how thoroughly you researched the firms to which you wrote.

And even if your resume does succeed in arousing the interest of a recruiter, don't necessarily expect a call right away. First, if the recruiter doesn't happen to be working on a search for which you would be a possibility, he has no immediate reason to call. Second, who has time to respond personally to all those resumes, anyway?

However, you *will* hear if the recruiter happens to be working on a search for which you may prove either a potential candidate or a helpful source. Though that may happen right away, it also may not happen for months to come.

The best that you can hope for—particularly from the largest firms—is that your resume will go into the computer data bank, where it will be ready to be retrieved when a search that fits you comes across a recruiter's desk.

If you decide to follow up sending your resume with a phone call, therefore, don't expect much more than a polite version of, "Don't call us, we'll call you."

"The worst kind of phone call is someone saying, 'I'm just checking to see if you received my resume,'" Jeanne Marie Gilbert says. "Well, I assume the U.S. mail works, and so of course I received it. It's a waste of time for both of us."

Open-ended questions might work better: "I wonder if you've had the opportunity to read my resume and if you could give me some feedback." That *will* work, Gilbert says, if the recruiter or researcher knows you from an earlier conversation or meeting. But remember: Given the volume of resumes coming across a recruiter's desk, unless your resume truly is memorable, don't expect the mere mention of your name to set the recruiter in motion on your behalf.

FOLLOWING UP 102: BY MAIL

It's difficult to keep sending letters to people you may have never met, knowing that you should not expect a response. Nonetheless, that's just what recruiters suggest you do: Periodically write them letters keeping them—and their computers —up-to-date on your activities.

Follow up, recruiters say, by periodically sending updated resumes: Have you been promoted? Have you switched jobs? Did you receive an industry award? What about that speech you gave at an industry convention? Or that article about industry marketing trends in which you were quoted? Perhaps the recruiter would find the thoughts expressed in that paper or article of interest.

Once again, don't necessarily expect an acknowledgment. Just keep on updating when appropriate. The computer will remind the recruiter that you exist.

SITTING TIGHT UNTIL THE CALL COMES

But *do* you have to sit tight and wait for the recruiter to call you?

It seems so unfair, when you have already done so much: You have joined organizations and contributed your services; you have volunteered to work on community projects and given speeches; you have widened your network and kept it in good repair; you have researched the firms and identified the ones that are the best matches for you; and finally, you have sent them your resume.

But recruiters, like most people, don't take kindly to being bugged or nudged. In fact, some recruiters go so far as to say that if you've done *your* job well—including the job of becoming visible—then you should have confidence that they will do *their* job, too. And often they will.

But there is also something more you can do:

Make yourself known to recruiters as a possible source. Someone who can help *them*.

Let us proceed to the next chapter, where we will learn all about how to do just that.

4

CULTIVATING THE HEADHUNTERS: HOW TO HELP THEM SO THAT THEY CAN HELP YOU

When you return from lunch, the pink message slip is waiting for you: "Joy Hunter from Hunter Associates." You recognize the name immediately. She's a recruiter specializing in your industry. She has worked with several of your colleagues, and you met her once at a professional association meeting at which she spoke.

It's flattering that she called, of course, but you wonder what she wants. Does she have a job possibility she thinks is appropriate for you, or does she only want to speak to you as a source for other names? In either case, you're nervous: This is a stranger, after all, and what if your boss finds out you're talking to someone about another position? Are you really *that* interested in looking somewhere else?

And even if you do listen, but decide the position is not for you, what if she then asks you to suggest other people who might be interested instead? What if you feel uncomfortable providing your colleagues' names and telephone numbers to someone you don't really know? Worse, what if the headhunter asks questions, and personal questions at that—about your salary, about how much you *really* like your job, or about your long-range plans, all subjects you feel you'd hardly want to broach with someone you've barely met.

And so the pink message slip stares at you and you stare

back. Do you return the call? Do you let it drop? And if you do call back, how do you behave? Do you act cold or friendly, distant or warm? Interested or not? Helpful or not?

Your eyes glance at the other messages waiting to be answered, all lined up in a row. It's such a busy afternoon, you think. Maybe, you say to yourself, you'll let her call you back instead. . . .

But wait a minute. What do you have to lose by dialing the number? Maybe the recruiter has something that would interest you. Maybe she's working on a search for which you would not be able to come up with any names even if you wanted to. Or maybe—just maybe—five minutes of conversation now might lead to a better-sounding possibility next month or next year. If you don't pick up the telephone, you realize suddenly, you just won't know.

So why not call back, you think?

Why not, indeed?

Calling back—or accepting the initial call—is often the very first step toward cultivating the headhunter so that the headhunter will cultivate you. Trading favors is another name for this game: Be a friendly source to the recruiter today, and on another day she'll remember you and call again. These calls may be further sourcing calls, or they may concern an opening suitable for you. Or, if you have hired recruiters in the past to hire people for you, but now find your own job on the line, you can make a call to ask a favor of your own.

In both cases, the barter is based on the creating and building of relationships. So let's look further into the two main ways to build relationships with recruiters—by hiring one or by becoming a source to one.

BUILDING BY HIRING

Hiring a recruiter to perform a search for you provides an obvious opportunity to both research the industry and make yourself known to the specialists in your field. You will be doing all this from a position of power—as the one who hires and fires the recruiter.

In some companies, recruiters are chosen or recommended by the human resources department, particularly when the search is not at the very highest level. But as the hiring manager, you should involve yourself in the selection of the recruiter as much as possible for several reasons. First, if the recruiter is hiring someone who will work directly for you, you will want to make certain that the search consultant fully understands the position being filled. A good recruiter will similarly want to meet you to find out what you think would constitute a good fit. Obviously, you are looking for someone who impresses you with his or her professionalism and someone with whom you can work comfortably. Less obviously, in interviewing recruiters to work for your company, you are also interviewing them as recruiters who may one day help you.

Before hiring a recruiter, you should research and screen the firms thoroughly. Do so in much the same way that you would go about selecting firms to which you would write as a potential job candidate: Talk to your professional friends and colleagues, people in your professional associations, other executives in the company, and colleagues in the human resources department. Once you've gathered a list of firms that handle the kind of search you need conducted, call and ask for more information or for an initial meeting. Many of the questions you'll ask now will also be the same, but with a slightly different emphasis. Here are some good ones to pose:

How many searches have you performed in this area? You want to know if it's the recruiter's first search in this field, or his fiftieth. Experience alone should not determine your decision, however. Some recruiters—particularly those starting out or seeking to establish a relationship with a client—are eager to compensate for their lack of knowledge in a field by performing extraordinary research and working harder. Regardless of the recruiter's level of experience, always ask about his game plan.

Who are some of your clients? You'll want to call several

companies the firm has worked for as references.

How long have you been in business? Ask about the history of the firm and about the recruiter's background in the search business. Because of the high turnover of search firms, you want to verify its credibility.

How do you plan to identify potential candidates? Make certain that the recruiter has a clear plan for performing the search—and that he can do the needed research in an ethical fashion.

How long do you estimate the search will take? The answer usually will depend on the nature of the position to be filled. Wooing happily employed executives—and negotiating the right compensation package—may take longer than expected.

How many candidates do you generally present to a client? Again, the answer might depend on the difficulty of the search, but initially most recruiters present no more than three or four candidates. If, as the search progresses, none of these initial candidates is to your liking, it might be time to reassess the job description and go over, carefully, what you did and did not like about the candidates you saw.

What are your fees? What about expenses? The industry's average fee is somewhere between 30 to 33-1/3 percent of the total cash compensation, Janet Jones-Parker says, with some firms offering fixed fees. Set the percentage, the payment schedule, and the expenses at the start.

What happens if the executive you place doesn't work out and has to leave? Some firms will do a second search for no fee or a highly reduced fee if, for some reason, the person hired leaves within a certain period of time. Julian-Soper, a Chicago-based retainer-search firm specializing in the insurance industry, promises to refill the position free of charge if the executive leaves within the first year; if the executive leaves during the second year, the firm will refill the position for half its normal fee. Some firms may be just as generous; with other firms, the grace period may be six months or less.

Once the search is completed, how long will my company— and what parts of my company—will be considered off limits to your firm? Similarly, what companies will be off limits to you when you do this search for my company?

All well and good, you say, if you *can* hire someone through a recruiter. But what if you're not in a position, or don't have the budget, to use executive-search firms? How else do you build relationships?

You become a source. A resource *to* the recruiters.

TRADING FAVORS: THE RECRUITER'S RESOURCE

What goes around, comes around. From the executive recruiter's point of view that might mean, help me now, and I'll help you later. *Don't* help me now, and later—well, we'll see.

No, not every recruiter keeps a mental scorecard giving credits to those who have been helpful and debits to those who have not. And it's not a calculated business game in which every favor given is *only* given with the expectation that one will be received in turn.

But put yourself in the recruiter's shoes for a minute and think about it. Whom would *you* remember, and *how*: the person who returned your phone calls, or the person who did not?

And in life in general, who would make the better impression—the person willing to listen and respond to your calls, or the one who remembers that she knows you only when she suddenly needs something from you? So call it trading favors or mutual backscratching, but by becoming a helpful source to a recruiter, you not only help him, you may also help yourself.

HOW NOT TO BECOME A RESOURCE

"Hello, Ms. Jones, this is John J. Recruiter from Recruiter Associates, and—"

"I'm sorry, Mr. Recruiter, I'm really not interested. Goodbye."

Click.

"Ms. Smith, my name is John J. Recruiter from Recruiter Associates. A Fortune 500 company has retained me to identify candidates for a position in your area and I'm wondering if I might speak with you for a—"

"I'm really tied up right now and just don't have a minute to spare. Sorry!"

Click.

"Hello, I'm John J. Recruiter, returning your call," the speaker introduces himself to me. "You say you're writing a book about women and executive search? Well, I want you to tell me why so many women just don't know how to handle a headhunter's phone call!"

DO WOMEN HAVE TROUBLE ANSWERING HEADHUNTERS' PHONE CALLS?

Are there differences between the way men and women handle recruiters' initial phone calls, interviews, negotiations, or other aspects of the job search? In the course of researching this book, I heard so many anecdotes from so many recruiters that I began to wonder, how many even highly placed executive women either do not understand the executive-search system or do not feel comfortable working with recruiters?

Some recruiters, including Allan Stern of Haskell and Stern, say that these gender-based differences amount to "a bunch of hogwash." Male or female, it makes no difference, he says. His firm looks for the "savvy executive"—and there aren't particularly more savvy executives belonging to one sex or the other.

Other recruiters make equally fervent comments on the other side of the issue. Because of the sensitivity of the subject, many recruiters were at first hesitant to discuss the subject— or agreed to talk only if they were promised anonymity.

"The women tend to be either extremely helpful or not helpful at all," one recruiter says, echoing the comments of others. "There doesn't seem to be as much of a middle ground."

"I started out specializing as a recruiter who placed women," another confides, "but I soon switched to placing men, too, because I had so much trouble finding women who knew how to play the game. And let's face it—you must play the game. That is the way life is."

"I think women tend to be loners—they don't know how to network as well as they should," another comments. "They don't know how to use a headhunter's call to network"—in other words, as a way to help both themselves and their colleagues.

"I just wish women in the interview process were a little bit more forthcoming and more natural and a little more at the level of security and confidence," a partner at one of the country's largest firms says. "I wish that they were just as candid and open as men are. Most men are open." The recruiter pauses thoughtfully and continues, "I'm not so sure that I could say that for most women."

Just how valid are these criticisms? Are these perceived differences between men and women based on reality or on cultural stereotypes? And if and when such differences do crop up, do we read more into them?

Here are my conclusions:

- Because women are still so far outnumbered by men in most executive offices, *any* deviation from what is considered to be the behavioral norm is highlighted.

  Say a recruiter calls eight men and two women as potential candidates for a position. One man refuses to cooperate; so does one woman. Half of the women didn't play the game, but only a very small percentage of the men did not.
- Because women are still new to higher-level executive positions, they are also new to headhunters' phone calls. As John Dugan, president of the National Association of Executive Recruiters, points out, "The first-time user of a search firm is naive to begin with, someone who does not know how to 'play the game.'"

Alice Early, a managing director at Russell Reynolds, makes a similar point. In the past, when women were just starting to reach higher-level positions, they may have been more reticent about talking to recruiters, she believes. But she also finds that to be much less the case these days.

- Because women are still new to higher-level executive positions, they are still in the process of developing a comfortable business style. The awkwardness that reciuters note may be a reflection of this.

There is some research to validate this theory. A study of executive women conducted by the Center for Creative Leadership in Greensboro, North Carolina, found that women have more difficulty adapting to the work environment than men. This "discovery" may not sound surprising, yet for women who have struggled to find a comfortable behavioral style within a company whose executives are mostly male, it is also validating.

"For women who are still paving the way in high-level jobs, the struggle to adapt may prove considerably more difficult than for men because in addition to trying to break stereotypes about what women can do, they may have to forge a personal style that seems neither too aggressively masculine nor too traditionally feminine," comments Ann M. Morrison, who directed the center's study.

This narrower band of acceptable behavior for women within the corporation creates a double-edged sword for many women, she says. Behave like a man, and you're being too aggressive, women are told; but behave like a woman, and—well, you're just acting like a woman.

- Because (as the Center For Creative Leadership study of executive women also found) women tend to receive less feedback about their job performance than men do, women executives simply may not be aware that they are making or have made certain missteps—among them, missteps involving responses to recruiters.

And if, as the study suggests, women tend to receive less

information from bosses and colleagues about how well they are doing, how others perceive them in the corporation, and what they might do in order to change or improve those perceptions, how can they correct mistakes they don't know they're making, or polish skills they aren't aware need some final finishing touch?

The study's message seems clear: Get more feedback— from your boss, peers, and other colleagues—and listen to what they say. If headhunters are any indication, you'll hear quite a bit.

- In the same way that many women must struggle to discover what the "band of acceptable behavior" is in their particular company, some may also need to fine-tune their career management skills.

  "It's a matter of being so work oriented that some women don't think of the value of taking ten to fifteen minutes out of a day to be cordial and helpful with the thought that that person might remember them some day when they have an assignment," suggests Sydney Reynolds. When it comes to the future, she says, "they have tunnel vision."

  A number of executive women agree with this assessment: "The more you keep your head down and worry about your own job, the more perspective you lose about where you're going," a manager at a high-tech company asserts. "When you finally lift your head up, you're not positioned, you're entrenched where you are. People don't know what you're interested in next, and when you try to tell them at that point, it just doesn't make an impression." This lesson, she says, was learned all too well from her own experience. At her new position—in which she was placed by a recruiter— "I'm letting people know what I'd *like* to do in the future, not just what I'm doing now."

  One of the career management skills still to be fine-tuned, many recruiters suggest, is knowing how to effectively answer their phone calls.

Another such skill, they suggest, is learning how to trade favors:

From the personnel manager of a health care management company: "My whole background is in helping people and doing things for others, but quite frankly I can't think of a time when I've had to call a favor in." From a Boston-based management consultant: "That's not something I do." From an executive in a New England insurance company: "The only favor I can recall asking someone to do for me was right before I went on a vacation, when I asked a colleague to water my plant."

One reason behind this discomfort in asking for a favor may lie with the very history of women in the workplace. "In the past, women weren't used to [trading favors]," says Eleanor Raynolds, a partner at Ward Howell, International. "We had the idea that we could do everything ourselves." And as Ladd Wheeler, Ph.D., professor of psychology at the University of Rochester, points out, for some people having to ask for something—anything—"is an admission that you can't do it all yourself."

Although many women felt in the past that they had to prove just how self-sufficient they were by never asking anyone for anything, recruiters point out that it is time to accept the fact that trading favors—asking as well as giving—is a time-honored part of American business life.

Some women also express discomfort with the idea of swapping favors, tit-for-tat. Of course, the more altruism involved in performing a favor, the better we feel. But, alas, business does not run on good deeds alone.

Is there something wrong with trading favors? A favor, after all, is nothing more than that—a favor. Bribes and other tainted acts are something else entirely.

Finally, being part of what one executive calls the "favor loop" may yield other benefits: "When people call me, I consider it an honor because it means that I have some power, or some information, that they would find useful," comments Sydney Reynolds. "By the same token, it leaves an open door for me to pick up the phone and call on those same people."

What goes around, comes around: It's a saying that recruiters and their sources live by.

BECOMING A RELIABLE RESOURCE

Why do recruiters love good sources? The answer is simple:

"Contacting people with whom I work in the industry and asking, 'Can you give me the name of someone you know to call, and may I use your name in talking to that person?'—that is the best way to find people," says Gracemarie Soper, president of Julian-Soper & Associates in Chicago.

"If you hit the right source, that's your research, that's your reference check, and that's your candidate identification all right there," Jeanne Marie Gilbert concurs. A good source, she says, can help do her search for her. It's no surprise, then, that good sources are not forgotten. "If a name comes up from nine years back, I can tell you if that person was a good source or not," Gilbert says.

And when you, as a known source, call to ask a favor in return—"I need your help and your advice, can I sit down with you for breakfast or a drink?"—don't worry. The trade-in will be honored.

How do you become a source? First, as outlined in the previous chapter, you make yourself visible, a person whose name will be mentioned when the recruiter begins looking for people in your particular area of expertise.

Second, when the recruiter calls, you must be prepared to listen. And even if the position he is calling about is not right for you, as long as the recruiter is reputable and knowledgeable, volunteer to be helpful. Suggest possible candidates or other sources. If you can't think of anyone offhand, offer to call back later—and then do so.

Finally, comments Thomas H. Ogdon, managing partner of the Ogdon Partnership in New York, "You've got to be someone who knows who good people are. You've got to have that as one of your skills." You've got to know who the people are in the industry, Ogdon says; who the *good* people are, and what they're doing. Being a source, in short, is one more job that is not designed for the loner.

NAMING NAMES

"All a source is doing is naming the people who are good in his or her field," Thomas Ogdon explains. "I call you up and say, 'Who are the good editors? Who are the *really* good editors?' And you say, 'Let me put down my work for an hour and tell you everything I know!'

"And then, after you hang up, you sit and think hard and go through your Rolodex again, and call back the next day and say, 'I forgot a really important name—he does such-and-such. He knows everything about an area I myself know nothing about. Call him and he'll tell you everything I don't.' Now that's a good source," Ogdon says, "provided that what the source tells you is for real."

The person Ogdon describes is not only a good source, but an ideal source—someone who always has more than enough time to tell the recruiter all, and all she tells is valuable.

But even ten or fifteen minutes can be enough time to establish a cordial relationship with a recruiter—if you know how to do it. According to Sydney Reynolds, the script for such a conversation need be no more complicated than this:

"Hello, I've been retained by XYZ Company to conduct a search, and I wonder if I could talk with you about it?"

"Well," you respond, "I'm quite happy where I am, but I'll listen to what you have to say."

The recruiter goes on to describe the job, but even after the first few sentences you know you're not interested. Let her finish, though—you do want to know what you're saying no to. Then say, "I don't think it's right for me, but let me think about it, and I'll get back to you with the names of a couple of people who might be."

And that may be the opening the headhunter has been looking for: "Well, tell me a little about *you*, then," the recruiter says. "What *would* be right for you?"

The next time she calls, she'll know.

Caution: Before revealing information that you would rather not, ask the recruiter to tell you a little bit more about *her*: "Are you a retainer or a contingency firm? Do you specialize in a particular area? What kinds of searches do you do, at what salary level, and at what level of job responsibility? Are you working on a particular search now, or just talking to people for whom you might have openings? Why is this job opening now? What kind of a company is it?"

Such questions need not be framed in a confrontational manner. Ask them in the context of trying to learn more in order to be able to help the recruiter: "The more you can tell me about your firm and your client, the better able I'll be to think of just who the right people might be." If you've told the recruiter you intend to call back, that will also give you time to see if colleagues are familiar with his or her firm, or for you to do any other checking.

Then, once you've determined that the recruiter really does have a position to fill and works for a reputable firm, it's time to continue the conversation: "Well," the recruiter repeats, "now tell me about you."

"And sometimes it could be just two things they tell me," Reynolds explains. "And I'll say, 'Well, if that changes, I'll get back to you. In the interim, if you think of someone for me, please call me.' It's an immediate exchange."

There. You're on the headhunter's list. Particularly if you *do* call back with leads.

THE "GOOD" SOURCE

But what kind of leads? The best lead is one that brings the recruiter right to the candidate who wins the job. Very often the recruiter will write on the close-out-sheet—that's recruiter's jargon for the summary page that ends up on the top of the file of a completed search—who the source for the candidate was: You.

"It doesn't matter how *often* you were a source—it's how good a source you were," Jeanne Marie Gilbert emphasizes.

And a "good" source can be defined quite simply: one who is on target.

Perhaps most important, good sources will qualify their information, Gilbert continues. They'll say, "X is good. Y is very good. Z is not the right person for this—the chemistry won't work."

Another favor for which the recruiter will be indebted to you is passing along an industry or association directory to which he would otherwise not have access. (Be careful that the person to whom you give the directory is someone you would want to trust with it, however.) If you *then* go through the directory with the recruiter, qualifying each name, you will surely remain in that recruiter's Rolodex for life.

As you name the names, the recruiter will ask, "When I call X, can I use your name?"

What do you say? If you feel uncomfortable letting X know you've passed along his or her name, simply say no. But if you say yes, you may gain some good will from the person whose name you mention.

Rather than immediately providing the recruiter with information, some sources will momentarily hold back. "Let me call a few people I might have in mind and see what they have to say. I'll call you back in a day or two," they'll say. They then use their position as a source to act as a kind of favor broker to others.

"They'll call up three friends and say, 'Hey, I've heard of a job—do you think you'd be interested?'" Gilbert explains. "Then they'll call me back and say, 'I have two guys who are all prepped and ready for your call.' The source is acting as a search person himself! And it works in his favor. Because then when you think of him, automatically he's high on the list as both source *and* candidate." Not coincidentally, he also will appear high on the lists of the three people whose names he passed along.

Even if you don't know, can't think of, or don't feel comfortable mentioning the names of potential candidates, you can be helpful in still other ways: Do you know someone else who might be familiar with people who would fit this search? Can you think of particular firms—or types of firms—where the recruiter might find the kind of candidate for whom he is looking?

Finally, tell the recruiter what areas you could be of help with in the future: "I've worked in X, Y, and Z banks, and still have good contacts there." When another search comes along, you'll hear from the recruiter.

SUSPECT SOURCES

As much credit as you earn for being a good source, however, you risk being discredited for being a *suspect* source. It's not that you yourself will be considered suspect. But if the information you provide is biased, inaccurate, or in other ways off the mark, what does that say about your judgment as a whole? Beyond repeatedly passing on tips that just don't pan out, recruiters cite two red flags:

* Are you providing the best information possible—or only trying to help a friend?

    Jeanne Marie Gilbert, for instance, admits she finds herself growing wary when a woman recommends *only* other women. The suspicion aroused is that the executive's judgment is biased, that her vision is limited to her friends alone, rather than open to the best people available. And even though this impulse might be borne of a zeal to help other women climb the executive ladder, Gilbert says, "To my mind it is not appropriate to think in terms of who is qualified for the job in terms of, 'Is it a man or a woman?'"

The same red flag, of course, *should* be raised for men who recommend men. However, because men still outnumber women so greatly in executive suites, that same suspicion probably would not arise.

- Are you too eager to be considered as a candidate yourself?

A potentially good source might also find herself becoming a suspect source if she seems too eager to consider *herself* a candidate, Thomas Ogdon says. "Maybe I was calling that person as a source. I already knew she was overqualified. But I called because I also knew she was in an area where she knew who all the right players were. And all of a sudden I have a candidate on my hands who I *don't* want on my hands."

Instead of being considered a good source now, Ogdon says, you've just been demoted to being an "easy" candidate who does not know her own value within the industry.

WARNING: CHOOSE YOUR CONFIDANTS CAREFULLY

You do not wish to be considered a suspect source; even more important, however, you do not wish to provide information to a *suspect recruiter.*

In the same way that you carefully choose the headhunters to whom you wish to be known, you should also choose those for whom you wish to be a source:

- Beware of the "funny phone calls" referred to in Chapter 3. Watch out for the caller who hesitates, neglects, or refuses to identify himself or herself.

- If the position described by the recruiter sounds suspect—
  the details are vague or it just sounds too good to be true—be
  on guard. Some researchers or recruiters go on fishing
  expeditions to get information about the people who work
  in a given company. Make sure a job opening actually exists.
  One way to do that is to ask questions about it: Why is this
  job opening? Why did the previous person leave and where
  did he go? To whom would the person in this job report?
  What is the company's structure? What is the company's
  corporate culture? What is the company's position in the
  marketplace relative to mine? Good recruiters will be as
  specific as possible.

  Sometimes, however, in order to protect a client's
  confidentiality, the recruiter legitimately cannot tell you
  many details about a position. But if he cannot tell you
  enough to satisfy a basic job description, you may well begin
  to wonder if an actual position exists.
- If the recruiter and his firm are not known to you, ask for
  information. Is the firm retainer or contingency? How long
  has it been in business? Does the firm specialize in a
  particular function or industry?
- Is the recruiter handling positions at the salary range and
  level of responsibility appropriate to *your* (and your
  colleagues') salary range and level of responsibility? Does
  the recruiter work on searches in your industry or function?
  If the answer is no to all of these questions, you might well
  ask, how and why did the recruiter decide to call you?
- Has the recruiter answered your questions sufficiently to
  convince you that he or she is someone you can trust when
  you or your colleagues ask for confidentiality? It's not only
  your resume you may wish to protect. You also may prefer to
  remain an anonymous source, a perfectly acceptable stance
  when you don't want so-and-so to know that you know that
  he knows that you know that he may be looking for a job....

When asking your questions, be courteous but be firm. You
have as much right to ask your questions as the recruiter has

to ask hers. After all, in an initial conversation, you are screening him as much as he is screening you.

And if you aren't satisfied with the answers you receive, then politely say you're not interested as a candidate, nor can you think of anyone at the moment who would be. Remember that in naming other names, you are also putting your own name on the line.

THE PAYOFF: FAVORS YOU CAN ASK

You've been a helpful source, or you've worked well with the recruiter that you hired to conduct a search for you. You've built good relationships with at least one recruiter, maybe more. Your favor currency has been accruing interest in the bank. Now it's time for the payoff. How do you ask? What can you ask?

"The best headhunters have a distinct view of the transactional nature of what they're doing," Thomas Ogdon comments. "For every favor granted, a favor should be returned.... And it happens that one of the favors headhunters are in a position to give is time to people who are in one of those moments of their lives when they're trying to change jobs."

When that time comes, the three basic rules of trading in your favors are simple and easy to follow:

- Be straightforward about the purpose of your call. No need to be smarmy or apologetic; no need, either, to be demanding or defensive. The recruiter who feels his arm is being twisted may perform the favor this time, but don't expect anything further in the future.
- Be realistic in gauging just how much you can ask for in terms of the recruiter's time and contacts.
- Be sure that this headhunter is the right headhunter for you to be talking to. If he does not work on searches in your area or industry, as much as he may want to help you, his ability

to assist will be limited. One favor he can do for you, however, is refer you to a recruiter in his firm who does specialize in your area.

First, the phone call: "Tom, I need your help and your advice. I understand I may not fit any of the searches you're working on right at this moment, but can we sit down for breakfast or a drink?"

This is the primary favor for which you can ask, some personal attention and time, a few minutes to tell the recruiter what you're looking for and to remind him to think of you when an appropriate search does cross his desk.

Can you ask for anything more than that?

It depends. If you are a former client or have had a particularly strong business relationship in the past, the recruiter may give you leads from his Rolodex or mention that he heard that a position was opening at XYZ Company. In doing this favor, the recruiter hopes to ensure that you call him the next time you have occasion to consider using a search firm.

In asking for a favor, be careful and don't overreach. Let the recruiter feel that he's being generous to you. The worst thing you can do is to make him feel that his arm is being twisted, that the favor is being extracted by force. Remember that part of the pleasure of doing someone a favor is having the opportunity to appear generous.

So let him feel generous—particularly if he is, and many will be. And after your meeting, follow up. Write a thank-you note. Let him know what happens with whatever advice, leads, or information he has provided. When you land a new position, let him know that, too.

OFF LIMITS: FAVORS YOU CANNOT ASK

Be direct—but don't be greedy. If you're tempted to overreach, remember that even if you get the favor this time, you should not expect another in the future. So be careful about what you ask for, and how you ask it. You might even get more than you expected.

Don't ask—and never expect—the recruiter to find a position for you on demand. We've already established that recruiters do not work this way, nor can anyone place an executive on demand.

Don't expect the recruiter to send you on interviews immediately; he may not be working on anything appropriate, so why waste everyone's time?

Don't expect the recruiter to refer you to recruiters in other firms. Some say they will on occasion; others say, "Does Macy's tell Gimbel's?"

Don't expect the headhunter to introduce you to potential employers with whom he is not currently conducting a search. "This is a favor I would do only for a very good client or for a very close friend and godfather to my children," Thomas Ogdon says.

If the recruiter works on contingency, he might be more likely to market you in this way, but many recruiters who work on retainer say they would seldom if ever agree to this favor, regardless of how strong the business relationship.

Why? Because such introductions can only put the retained recruiter in an awkward position with that client (or potential client). "Either you have to say, 'By the way, this is a freebie, there's no fee involved,' or you have to be indefinite about that because maybe you would take something," Ogdon comments. "Either way it's a little uncomfortable."

Apparently, though, this practice is not as uncommon as some recruiters claim. Even though a number of retainer firms frown on such transactions as being tainted with the aura of contingency work, at Handy Associates, for instance, an introduction between candidate and client given in this way is dubbed a "Sir Galahad."

POLISHING THE ART OF CULTIVATING: IN SUMMARY

And so, when a recruiter calls, remember the benefits of being helpful:

- As a source you have the opportunity to present yourself in a different light from a job seeker. Instead of someone *asking* for something, you are someone with something to offer— information. You are presenting yourself as an equal, as someone with whom the recruiter can build a business relationship.
- A good source probably will find her way into both the recruiter's Rolodex and the firm's computer data base. That way, if the recruiter goes to another firm, your name goes with him—and still remains in the original firm's files.
- When it's time to switch jobs, you'll know one person more in a position to help, or at least give advice.

And when it's time to call in a favor, know who you're asking, know why you're asking, know what you're asking, and know what you *can* ask. Ask the appropriate questions well, and you're not likely to be turned down.

In short, cultivate the headhunter, and the headhunter will cultivate you. With this in mind, we turn to the etiquette of the chase itself.

5

WHEN THE CALL COMES:
THE ETIQUETTE
OF THE CHASE

The phone rings. The recruiter is on the line.

"I'm identifying potential candidates for a senior financial position at a Fortune 500 company, and I'm wondering if I could talk to you for a few minutes."

You think, happy are those who find themselves in demand!

Until it hits you: What do you do after you agree to listen?

THE RULES OF THE GAME

There is an appropriate order and etiquette for everything under the sun, including headhunting. There are rules and regulations for each and every stage of this hunt, from receiving the phone call to meeting the recruiter, for handling all those delicate questions about your personal life that might well be illegal, for interviewing (and being interviewed by) the client, for following up with the recruiter, for handling the rejection if you don't get an offer and for negotiating the best deal if you do get one, for deciding whether to move on in your career or for the moment to just stay put, and finally, for breaking the news to the parties concerned.

The chase has begun. Let's go.

THE PHONE RINGS...

...And the headhunter is on the line. You know all the reasons you should take a moment to listen, but what should you be listening *for?*

Listen carefully and the caller's pitch will contain most of the cues and clues you'll need:

"Hello, I've been retained by a Fortune 500 Company to identify someone..."

Retained. You know it's a retainer firm.

"Hello, my client has asked me to identify candidates for a senior financial position..."

Identified. No mention of retainer. It's probably a contingency firm.

"Are you interested?"

You're a potential candidate.

"What are your thoughts?"

You're potentially a candidate or a source. The headhunter hasn't made up his mind yet, and neither have you.

Of course, you have taken note already of your caller's name and the name of his firm. Perhaps you recognize the firm as a well-known one specializing in your industry; perhaps you know the recruiter's name because he placed a colleague or was hired once by a friend in another company.

Or perhaps you don't recognize the name at all. It's time to ask a few questions more. After all, since the recruiter is trying to get information from you, it's only fair to ask for the information you need from him to:

- decide if you are interested in the position
- determine if you can be a helpful source
- make certain that the recruiter is reputable and someone you do want to help.

And so you say: "I'm sorry. I didn't catch the name of your firm. Could you tell me a little bit more? Are you a retainer or a contingency firm? Do you specialize in a particular industry or area?"

There's even more you should know: "How well do you know the client? Is this your first search for the client? Your second?"

Whether the recruiter is working on contingency or retainer, the better he knows the client, the more information he should be able to provide about the particular job in question. A client with whom a recruiter works repeatedly also indicates the client's confidence in the recruiter.

After you've settled these points, ask even more specific questions about the job: "What's the environment like at this company? Why is there an opening? Why did the other person leave and where did he go? What do you see as the positives as well as the negatives about this particular job?"

And as you're asking these questions, don't forget to ask: "What's the compensation?"

Although this may sound like an obvious question, apparently it is also one that some otherwise savvy executives seem reluctant to ask. "It's interesting to me that women will frequently get a lot of information and reveal more than they should when talking about a job for which they don't know the compensation," says Dee A. Soder, Ph.D., a former recruiter who is now the president of the New York-based executive assessment and counseling firm, Endymion. Soder once inadvertently called an executive making $350,000 a year about a job that paid $200,000. The candidate, Soder says, "spent a lot of time on the phone talking about it, and when she found out the compensation, she was embarrassed. We could have saved each other a lot of time."

Whether your current salary is $40,000 or $450,000, however, make certain that the position's compensation and level of responsibility are enough to entice you. But even if you're not interested in being a candidate, you may still wish to offer help as a source.

Have you heard enough to make a decision already? "I don't think this is the position for me, but let me see if I can come up with some names of people who might be interested."

Or perhaps you are interested: "I'm perfectly happy where I am, but I'd be willing to meet and talk with you further." (Don't sound too enthusiastic yet; being a little hard to get will make you that much more attractive.)

Or perhaps you're still not certain: "Thank you for calling," you say to conclude the conversation. "Let me think about what you've told me and I'll get back to you."

And then do.

Aim in this initial exchange, Soder says, to stay in control of the conversation. Do so by asking questions and making sure you find out the information that you need to know. Don't be so controlled or aggressive that you scare away a potentially helpful recruiter. But remember: "You can find out an awful lot in those first ten minutes," Soder points out—if you know how. So don't be a passive partner to the conversation. Ask questions and get the information you need. Balance your interest with a healthy skepticism and see what happens next.

IF YOU CAN'T TALK IN THE OFFICE...

Perhaps, when the call comes, you're on a deadline and have no time to spare. Perhaps there's someone in your office. Perhaps you're in an open office, where there is no door to close.

Or perhaps there's even more of a constraint. It's not only that you like your current job and have no intention of moving. Some firms—and some bosses—frown upon their people talking to recruiters. They see it as a sign of disloyalty and count it as a mark against you. Their concern runs deeper than anxiety over losing one good person, however; it's the chain reaction they fear. Once a key executive or two from the department finds greener pastures somewhere else, they worry, won't the others look for those same pastures, too?

Some recruiters, sensitive to these issues, leave only first names when they call, or false names, or their real names without the firm's name, or won't leave messages at all. But as one executive who is frequently called points out, "You can always tell who those callers are, anyway." No one can control incoming calls; it's the calls that you accept—or return—that can cause concern.

Perhaps, for these reasons, closing the door when the recruiter calls does not seem safe enough for you. After all, your office door is never closed. Just seeing it shut will be a signal to your colleagues that something is going on. And though the recruiter promises to respect your need for confidentiality, you're still wary.

But you're also somewhat interested.

So you simply say: "I'm sorry, I can't talk right now. May I give you a call at home this evening?"

If the recruiter is interested, he'll say yes.

"That will also allow you to check them out a little bit," Soder says. (Of course, you have written down the recruiter's name, the firm's name, and the telephone number, so that you can find out more information.)

Then, if you do meet with the recruiter, arrange to do so in an informal setting—for breakfast or a drink after work—rather than at the recruiter's office.

SHOULD YOU TELL YOUR BOSS?

In contrast to bosses who frown when their employees even answer a recruiter's phone call, there are other executives who take it as a sign of pride that their staff members are being sought. "My staff is always being hunted, and I'm always competing with some very tough headhunters," Martha Green comments. "But I've always had a point of view—even when I was a campaign manager and losing staff constantly—that a job isn't going to fit someone forever. So my staff is very straight and open with me about that."

Further, in some offices, executives simply assume their staff members are receiving calls. The industry, company, or specialty is so hot, that they feel there would be something wrong if their people weren't getting calls.

One executive was so open with her boss about her job-hunting activities that she chastised the recruiter with whom she was negotiating a final job offer for not giving his real name when he called. "I was consulting with my boss about how to negotiate the deal. He knew everything. There was no need for secrecy."

But other bosses may take the news that you're job hunting more personally. And because a single phone call is a far cry from a solid offer, why put the suggestion in your boss's head that you're more serious about leaving than you perhaps are, or that your departure is more imminent than you would like it to be?

In still other cases, you may use the recruiters' calls as a means of broaching the subject of your future. After receiving several tempting calls, one publishing executive set an appointment with her boss to discuss what opportunities he—as well as she—saw in store for her if she remained in place. The meeting helped them to crystallize her position within the organization, and less than a year later she received a promotion.

In short, there are so many possible situations that there are no set guidelines, except for this: before saying anything, make sure you know your boss.

IF YOU CAN TALK, BUT YOU'RE NOT SURE HOW INTERESTED YOU ARE—OR HOW INTERESTED YOU SHOULD BE

What if you have no problem talking in the office, but after an initial conversation you're still not sure how interested you are? You've learned a lot in those first ten minutes on the telephone, but you still have questions about the recruiter or the job or both. What do you do?

One thing you can do is ask to see a written description of the job, what the recruiters call the job specification or "spec." Most recruiters will agree to send you something. How detailed the description is, however, will depend on how serious a candidate you seem to be. For some searches, in fact, a spec sheet will be mailed to prospective candidates *before* any calls are made. The recruiter will call afterward to follow up.

Of course, if there is no job description—because no job exists—by asking to see something in writing, you will get the answer to another question, too.

Asking to see something in writing will also give you more time to research the headhunting firm. Are your friends familiar with the recruiter or his firm? If so, what were their experiences?

What if you can't find a listing for the firm, and your friends never heard of it? No cause for alarm in itself. In recent years many recruiters from the larger firms have split off to form small firms of their own. These firms may be so new that they will not be listed in any of the directories; that is all the more reason to get some information from the recruiter about his background and his firm before you hang up. But if the recruiter hems and haws when you ask about his background, you may have cause to wonder.

You can even ask the recruiter for client references. "I check their references," recruiter Allan Stern says, "why shouldn't they check mine?"

Take the time to check out the firm. But if you tell the recruiter, "Let me think about it and get back to you," regardless of your answer, as a courtesy, you should. You never know when you'll want to count that recruiter as a friend.

ARE YOU A CANDIDATE OR A SOURCE?

As you listen to the job description, do you see yourself as a candidate or a source? Since you will handle the phone call differently depending on the role in which you have been cast (or decide to cast yourself), it's important to establish the nature of the call from the start.

Ask directly, "Are you calling me as a candidate or a source?" Sometimes—particularly if the caller has not spoken to you before—the recruiter himself may not know. But as you hear more about the position, and he hears a bit more about you, the answer should become clear.

CULTIVATING THE CALLER: TURNING THE CALL INTO A SOURCING CALL

You've established who the caller is, you've thought about the opening, and now you've made your decision. This job is not quite right for you, but you would like the headhunter to keep you in mind for future jobs. At this point, it's to your mutual benefit to turn the call into a sourcing call.

Be direct: Tell the caller that the job isn't a good fit for you and why. As you speak, he'll be scribbling down everything you say. Next, offer some suggestions as to who would be a good fit. If you can't come up with names, suggest companies. But make sure that the suggestions are appropriate. Your credibility is only as good as your suggestions are. If you need or want time to think about those suggestions, offer to call back when you've had an opportunity to go through your Rolodex.

One favor that will put the recruiter in your debt is to offer to pass on an industry list or association directory. Recruiters and researchers live and die by such lists—feed them some, and they'll always come back to you.

Finally, close the conversation with the future in mind. "I hope you'll think of me again. Let me know if I can be of help the next time something comes up." You might also suggest the possibility of meeting at some unspecified time in the future, Dee Soder advises. "If there's no reason for it, the recruiter will say no. Nothing ventured, nothing gained."

POTENTIAL TURNOFFS THAT SHOULD NOT TURN YOU OFF

"And here was this total stranger asking me these personal questions that I thought were quite intrusive," the investment banker tells me. "Even if I did want to talk about how much money I made or how happy I really was—would I tell him?"

How dare the recruiter! a part of you says as the headhunter's questions pour out:

"What's your current compensation?"

"How old are you?"

"Do you feel satisfied with your current situation?"

And to add insult to injury, when you ask *him* a simple question about the client he is representing, you hear, "I'm sorry, but the search is confidential, and I cannot tell you my client's name."

Well!

But as intrusive as those questions may sound, and as uncommunicative as some of his replies might strike you, the recruiter is simply doing his job.

"In those first ten minutes, recruiters might ask you some fairly intrusive-sounding questions," Dee Soder admits. "They're only doing it because they want to qualify you as a candidate as quickly as possible. My recommendation would be to go ahead and answer them. If you feel uncomfortable, answer in a way that would indicate that you would answer at a later time."

Or, better still, Soder suggests, turn the situation around and ask the recruiter:

"What's my compensation? Well, what does the job pay?"

"How old am I? Well, what age range are you looking for, with how many years and what kinds of experience?"

If the recruiter cannot tell you the client's name, that should not be automatic cause for alarm, Soder says; rather, it may be an indication that the search is confidential, that the executive hasn't left the position in question yet, or that the position is new. In fact, she says, this might indicate a more interesting job. The company could be introducing a new product, starting an unusual marketing campaign, doing something new or unusual that you could play a role in shaping.

But even if the recruiter can't reveal the client's identity, he should be able to answer other questions: Why is this position open? What's the company's corporate culture? What are the politics like there? What's the company's position in the marketplace relative to your own company? What are the prospects for the future in this job that will make it more attractive than your current one?

Never be afraid to ask. By taking an active role in the conversation, you're doing more than protecting yourself. You're presenting yourself as someone who knows what questions are important. You're showing judgment and selectivity. Finally, if you don't ask what you need to know, who will?

SOME REAL REASONS TO BE TURNED OFF

As you go through your mental checklist deciding whether or not this is a job you would like to pursue or a headhunter you would like to meet, your impression can't help but be influenced by the salesman's pitch. For make no mistake, it is a sales pitch, and in the same way that there are salesmen who somehow always hit the right note, there are others who just sound off-key.

Although, as Howard Stevens puts it, "Headhunters are essentially harmless people," it's only playing it safe to make certain that your caller is a reputable recruiter with a bona fide search. Naturally, you begin to wonder about a caller who is clearly not familiar with your industry. If he doesn't understand the basic terminology, just how experienced is he? It's a matter of self-protection to ask to know more about the recruiter and his firm before going any further.

You should also beware of the hard-sell artist: the one who promises the best opportunity you ever heard; the one who asks for money up front for anything; the one who insists that you send him a resume before he tells you a thing.

If the recruiter does any of the above, be on guard.

MEETING THE RECRUITER

You say good-bye and hang up the phone; this was ten minutes well spent. You've qualified the recruiter, and the recruiter has qualified you. What comes next?

Perhaps you'll meet for breakfast, lunch, coffee, or a drink. Maybe you'd prefer to meet in the recruiter's office. But wherever you meet, make sure that you are comfortable with the arrangement: As mentioned earlier, some companies—and some executives—get more upset than others when they hear their staff members are speaking to recruiters. So be discreet. Choose the more informal setting—for a cup of coffee, perhaps—one that does not have the trappings of an "official" business occasion. As more than one executive points out, if all you're doing is having a drink with an interesting person, what's so disloyal about that?

Interviews with recruiters fall into two categories: those arranged to discuss a particular search and those known as courtesy interviews. The recruiter may extend this "courtesy" to you for a variety of reasons: He might be meeting you as a favor to you or to a mutual friend. Perhaps you are an executive who is in town only for the day. Or maybe the recruiter wants to meet you as a potential candidate for future searches.

The courtesy interview is usually far shorter than one based on a particular position; after all, without a specific position or company to discuss, there would be far less ground to cover. But though the kinds of questions asked might differ—a courtesy interview would remain much more general, obviously—rules of etiquette remain the same for either kind of interview.

But what are the rules?

Be comfortable, certainly, but not too comfortable. Even an informal meeting over drinks is serving the purpose of formally introducing you to a professional colleague.

Therefore, recruiters advise, dress, speak, and act like a professional, and prepare the way you would for any interview.

Professional dress or professional uniform? So much has been written about dressing for success, you'd think that this is one subject that need not be discussed. But some recruiters feel that the dress-for-success experts have done their job a bit too well.

"I remember working on a search in the financial area," a recruiter in one of New York's largest firms recalls, "and if you sat all the women I interviewed together in a conference room, I literally would not have been able to pick out one from the other. They had all read a book that told them how to dress, and they were all wearing suits—that's fine—but they were the most remarkably unattractive suits you could imagine: drab, mannish kinds of suits, with a white blouse, very severe hair styles, little or no makeup, no jewelry except for an inconspicuous watch and a wedding ring.

"All, that is, except for one or two women—and they were the ones I remembered. They also wore suits, but they wore ones that were becoming to them and that exercised their own sense of style. But it wasn't just style. They had a sufficient comfort level within themselves that told them they could wear this and be very professional. They had a sense of being in command of themselves; they didn't have to take the cookie-cutter approach."

Of course, dressing with too much flash or glitz is also a no-no. The woman who wears a fur coat to a meeting with a recruiter has ruled herself out of the job already. One head-hunter notes: "She's probably making more than me!"

What does "professional" behavior mean, anyway? Beware of appearing to be cut from the same mold as everyone else, recruiters warn. And yet they also say that women should avoid behaving in ways that seem either too buttoned-up or too informal, too personal or too aloof, too aggressive or not assertive enough. More women than men, they say, seem to have trouble finding a comfortable stance somewhere in between the two extremes.

Sound familiar? The recruiters' comments underscore a point made by the Center for Creative Leadership study of executive women discussed earlier: For executive women, the study found, there is a narrower band of acceptable behavior than for men. Perhaps the recruiters' comments also reflect the fact that most women just haven't played the business game long enough to discover how to sound the note that is proper and appropriate not just for women, but for themselves as individuals.

The recruiters' observations also emphasize another message implicit in the Center's study: The more feedback you can get about the ways in which others perceive you—about the way you perform in a business meeting or how you come across in an interview—the better able you will be to help discover what that right note is.

Professional homework. Prepare for this business meeting as you would for any other, recruiters advise. The advice sounds elementary—would you go into any other kind of business meeting unprepared?—but judging by the number of recruiters who emphasize this point, it also appears to be advice that often goes unheeded.

Prepare a list of questions you wish to ask or points you wish to make. If you already know the name of the client company, go to the library and read about it. Recruiters are quick to point out that just because the headhunter called you does not mean you are in for an easy interview. You passed the initial screening on the telephone, true. But you still have to prove yourself to get to the next cut. Further, you should be weighing whether or not this really is a position that would induce you to move. Would you go to any other job interview without a list of questions to ask about the company, the position, the prospects for the future it might hold?

The more thought you put into your presentation beforehand, the better impression you'll make, and the more confident and poised you'll sound. Dee Soder recalls the time she met with a candidate whom she felt would be a "stretch" fit at best for the job she was seeking to fill; but his thoughtful questions about the industry, the company, and the particular position convinced her to present him to the client after all.

Should you bring your resume? It depends. If your boss frowns on employees even speaking to recruiters, what must he think of a staff member actually submitting a resume? To get around that obstacle, Soder suggests providing the recruiter with a company biography or something that *looks* like a company bio. Further, since one purpose of the interview is to establish where you've worked, when, and in what capacity, having these facts in writing will save time. Instead of having to establish your work history, step by step, you can discuss other aspects of the position and delve more deeply into your work history.

If the search is contingency rather than retainer, be sure to check on the recruiter and his firm thoroughly before providing anything in writing. To further assure confidentiality, Janet Jones-Parker advises telling the recruiter that you will agree to go on client interviews *only* if the recruiter has called you first to get your approval to send a resume or present your name.

Follow-up: Whether the initial meeting leads to a client meeting or nothing at all, Soder advises sending a brief thank-you note. In addition to being common business courtesy, the note can be used to remind the recruiter that you would be happy to help as a source for future searches.

If, after this initial meeting, both you and the recruiter wish to pursue further discussions, then along with the thank-you note you might enclose your resume—if you did not present it before—along with whatever articles or speeches you may have mentioned in the interview that the recruiter and his client might find of interest. "Sending material in two tiers like that can have a very positive effect," Soder says. It gives you a further chance to reinforce your credentials and impress your candidacy on the recruiter's consciousness.

THE INTERVIEW ITSELF: BREAKING THE ICE

The recruiter greets you and ushers you into a comfortable chair. The inevitable "ice-breaking" chitchat that follows is designed to allow you to size each other up. Comment on the paintings on the wall, the decor of the office, a poster you spotted in the office lobby. You might find a mutual interest that will add another dimension to the interview and, perhaps, to your continued business dealings, whether you get this job or not. Further, by the time the *real* interview begins, you already have some idea of the person to whom you're talking.

There are as many interview styles as there are recruiters, and you may like this particular recruiter's style or you may hate it. You may find him cold or gregarious, aloof and impassive, overly formal or street-smart cynical, condescendingly patrician or engagingly talky. If his manner is congenial to you, all the better. But if it is not, beware: It is the easiest thing in the world to ascribe thoughts or feelings to a recruiter that just aren't there. It is the next easiest thing in the world to fall into the trap of responding to those ascribed feelings in ways that may not be to your advantage.

For instance, the engagingly talky recruiter may make *you* all too engagingly talky yourself—when you want to seem businesslike. The old-boy patrician recruiter might trigger a hostile reaction; or an unresponsive, stone-faced interviewer might set you on edge, wondering, How am I *really* doing? Be aware of these feelings and monitor them. Relax and try to be yourself, not a persona invented to please someone else's expectations.

"SO TELL ME ABOUT YOURSELF"

"So tell me a little bit about yourself," the recruiter says, and from the wave of his hand you know that the stage is yours.

How you respond is the first test of the interview.

Recruiters emphasize that although this is an invitation to speak, it is not a request for a one-hour monologue. "Even though the recruiter will ask you a lot of questions, don't misconstrue that the person is your best friend," Chris Stevens says. "They really don't want to hear every last detail." As in a debate, therefore, your opening remarks should extend for from five to ten minutes—no more than that and no less.

Because organization is crucial, Dee Soder suggests prefacing your remarks with a kind of outline: "Let me tell you about three areas—about my personal life, my management style, and my work experience." Lead with the personal—the brief, factual, cocktail-chat summary of your life—because it's the easiest thing to rattle off, Soder advises. "You also answer all those questions that are illegal to ask and that the recruiter wants to know." (More on how to handle these questions will appear later in this chapter.) With that out of the way, you can then stress your business style and, most important, your experience.

SOME QUESTIONS YOU MIGHT HEAR

Different recruiters may ask different questions in different ways, but their questions are all designed to elicit information about you and your experience, how you would or would not fit into a particular company or position.

During the years she worked as a recruiter, Dee Soder asked questions like the ones listed below. The questions are thorough and probing, reflecting Soder's training as a psychologist. As you read through the list, frame your own answers. Whether or not the recruiter who interviews you asks these particular questions, be prepared to answer similar ones. Your responses now should further help you to think more clearly about your career and life goals in general. After you've thought through your answers, you may begin to understand why executives often say that a good interview can help them crystallize their thoughts about both where they are now and where they would like to go in the future.

Here are Dee Soder's questions:

1. *What was your early life like? How do you think it has affected you?*

2. *Where did you go to school and why?*

3. *What kind of student were you in school?*

4. *What do you feel you got out of school?*

5. *Where did you work? What were your responsibilities? Your accomplishments? What lessons did you learn? What did you move from/to in each position?*

6. *Why were you successful (or unsuccessful) at each position?*

7. What are you most proud of? Least proud of?

8. Describe your management style. How does it differ from that of your boss?

9. Describe the ideal boss for you. What skills does your current boss have that you want to learn or emulate? What are the things about him that bug you?

10. Describe your current position. What are your responsibilities and accomplishments? Would you draw your organizational chart? [Be sure to draw superiors, lateral colleagues, and subordinates. Leaving out one tier says something about how you view yourself within the organization.]

11. Describe your current corporate culture.

12. Tell me about your ideal job: What would you like to do? For whom? What type of management? What would be your compensation?

13. What are your greatest strengths? Name your top three assets. What about your weaknesses? Is there a strength you use to excess?

14. What is a common misperception about you?

15. Do you have greater insight into yourself or others?

16. What type of job do you want to avoid?

17. What is your current compensation? How do you feel this compares to your peers? Who are your peers?

18. Why did you choose (sales, personnel, etc.) as a career?

19. What is the biggest mistake you ever made in business? How did you solve it?

20. What is the biggest risk you ever took in business? Was it successful? If so, why? If not, why not?

21. What is the biggest problem you have now, or have had in

the past, with a peer? With a boss? How was each problem resolved?

22. What three adjectives would your boss use to describe you? What three would peers use? Subordinates? Your spouse or "significant other"?

23. If you had $10,000 to use solely on your own development, what would you do?

24. What types of people seem to rub you the wrong way?

25. What are the key requirements for a successful executive? Specifically, what are the requirements within your company?

26. What do you think about how your industry is operating today? What direction do you think it should take?

27. What interests you about your company's product or services?

28. What do you feel determines a person's success?

29. What advice would you give your child or someone else's child about business?

30. How hard do you work?

31. How will you know when you've been successful?

32. Where do you get your drive?

33. What periodicals do you routinely read? What did you think about the recent cover story in ___ ?

34. How do you reward yourself?

35. How do you feel after you've accomplished a goal?

36. Outside of work, what gives you the most satisfaction?

37. What is your mission? How are you accomplishing that? What have been the results?

38. How did you increase sales, profits, etc.?

39. What frustrations or problems do you face in your current position?

40. What limitations have you overcome, and how?

41. When you assumed your last job, what goals, ambitions, and concerns did you have in mind?

42. What enduring mark will you (or did you) leave on your company?

43. Are there any questions that you'd like to ask?

As you delve more deeply into the position to be filled, the recruiter's questions will begin to focus on the specifics of the job itself: "What interests you about this position? About this company? About the type of work you would be doing there?"

In answering hypothetical questions—"What would you do if __ ?" or "How would you handle the responsibility of __ ?"—remember how you handled similar situations in the past: "Well, based on what I did when such-and-such happened, I would do the following..."

Although "trick" questions and stress interviews have gone out of fashion in recent years, some recruiters still use these techniques to test executives. If you come across a recruiter who is belittling or insulting, who just seems to be "asking for it," he probably is, as a means of seeing just how aggressive or assertive you are.

WHAT ABOUT ILLEGAL QUESTIONS?

Strictly speaking, it's illegal for a recruiter to ask any question that it would be illegal for an employer to ask—questions about a job applicant's age, religion, or national origin. Depending on the job and the way the question is asked, it may not be legal, either, to ask about whether or not you are married, plan to become pregnant, or expect to leave once you do have children in order to raise your family.

But most recruiters ask such questions—or encourage you to volunteer the answers—anyway.

And you can understand their reasoning: They want to see what Alice Early of Russell Reynolds describes as "the whole picture of what's on the candidate's mind" and the whole picture of who he or she is. Recruiters—like employers—want to make sure that the candidate "fits" the organization in terms of personality and style as well as in terms of work experience.

Further, as Carol Kanarek points out, "The very reasons people want to switch jobs very often have to do with these things." For instance, as part of a dual-career couple, an executive finds she has tired of commuting between New York and Chicago, and so she decides to look for a job in Chicago, where her husband works. Or, now that her children are in school, she's ready to take on a new challenge in her career. Further, as recruiters point out, it's not just women who make job moves for these reasons; men do, too.

"I ask the same questions, man or woman," Alice Early says, "who they are, what the family situation is, if they're married, or if this is the second marriage and they have children in Detroit.... If a person has been married several times, that's a fact. If a person has never been married, that's also a fact. It's just a piece of information that clients want to know. And I have never had a client not award a job to someone because of that kind of information."

Not only do most recruiters ask these questions of both men and women, they point out that the *reasons* for asking such questions of women are different today than before.

"Back in 1973, I'd have executives interview and say, 'Well, who is going to take care of the children?'" Janet Jones-Parker says. "If that question were asked today, it would be asked as a point of reference, of interest, as opposed to a reason for not selecting. The question would be about how you solve your problems. It's a very different context."

"I don't think that there are very many 'woman's' issues, to be very honest," Sydney Reynolds says. "I think they are issues. And they don't belong only to women. It's that women carry a little extra baggage on issues that have attached themselves to women."

The issues, of course, have to do with families. With dual careers. With combining parenthood—in particular, motherhood—with professional ambition. With having it all. With making compromises. With life itself.

And certainly, as Sydney Reynolds points out, these are issues that face men as well as women. But precisely because these issues do more often attach themselves to women than to men, they are *perceived* as women's issues, and must be addressed as such.

Further, so many articles have appeared in *The Wall Street Journal* and elsewhere focusing on women dropping out of the corporation in order to rear children that new doubts are being raised in some executives' minds. And recruiters like Allan Stern contend that the articles are reporting on reality. "Companies are finding that they are losing the middle-managment women who are deciding to take either six months or a year's leave of absence for family reasons," Stern comments. "And I see many women also either going into their own businesses or into smaller companies, or into industries which I think are going to be female dominated."

As a result of these dual trends—of women dropping out for family reasons and switching from large corporations to smaller businesses—Stern foresees "a whole new phenomenon. The 25 to 35-year-old group is going to have a harder time moving ahead in the corporate world" because of fear that they will drop out, and at the same time there will be a resurgence of interest in hiring women 40 and older, who already have their families in place.

That may be good news for some, but what if you're between the ages of 25 and 35 now and either have young children at home or plan to have kids soon? How do you frame the answers to the recruiter's questions—particularly if you aren't yet sure about the answers yourself?

Counselors advise that you answer the questions, but be prepared and answer well. Refusing to answer raises a red flag for the recruiter: why is she being defensive?

Listen to the tone in which the questions are asked. "If I were in an interview and a potential boss asked me about my child plans with the implication that I might not be available, I would really question whether that company was the right one for me," Alice Early says. "That kind of thinking would just turn me off."

In framing your answers, remember that however friendly the recruiter is, he or she is not a bosom buddy, but an employee of the hiring company. Be open if the question is asked —yes, you've been divorced—but don't take the recruiter through every messy stage that led up to or followed it. Similarly, instead of going through the difficulties you had finding child-care arrangements for the first six months after you went back to work, emphasize the stable arrangement you've established over the past two years.

"You have to trust the recruiter, but you should also be a little bit wary," Carol Kanarek warns. "Just remember who is buttering the recruiter's bread." The key, perhaps, is to be honest, but also be discreet.

There are other tactics. When questions about children and family come up, one executive found that humor defused the situation best: "I'm a lawyer, so when people ask me illegal questions I always say, 'Is this a test of my legal skills?' We both laugh and then I answer."

You can also take the approach of volunteering the information. For instance, when the recruiter asks, "What are your long-range plans?" or says, "Tell me about yourself," include something about your personal plans in a few concise, well rehearsed sentences.

If the recruiter or client is particularly wary about hiring women, the best defense might be a good offense, Kathleen Lusk Brooke says. "Take a double-whammy approach. If you are able to travel and work overtime, then you should say that right at the start because as a woman the interviewer will assume it's an issue."

In this sort of situation, volunteer the information yourself: "I know that whenever you see someone with children, there may be a question if there will be difficulties with overtime or travel. I want you to know that I have arranged the child care. That is no problem."

If overtime and travel are problems, volunteer that information also—but in the broader context of your career as a whole. "I'd be very interested in a traveling situation, and over time that would be no problem. But I'm pacing my career. Right now I think it would work out best if I were not traveling extensively. In the future, though, I would consider more travel."

Don't be overly defensive in bringing up these issues, however; that will make the interviewer wonder, too. Nonetheless, "You cannot pretend that these issues do not exist," Brooke says. "But by bringing it out in a positive, controlled way, you can play the situation to your advantage."

In investigating whether or not the position would be good for you, find out how other women have fared at the company. *Can* a woman succeed in this company? What has been the record of other women there? Have they been promoted or passed over? Is the corporate culture tough, macho, male dominated? Can you fit in if you prefer ballet to football? Will they be supportive if your family status changes? The more clearly you think through all these issues and questions beforehand, the more focused you will appear—someone who knows where she's going, both in terms of her career and in the larger framework of her life.

SOME QUESTIONS FOR YOU TO ASK

Remember Dee Soder's advice: Stay in control of the conversation. But with the recruiter asking so many questions of you, how can you? First, prepare the points you wish to make beforehand about your accomplishments, goals, and so on, and then find a way to make them in the course of the conversation.

Next, just as important, ask questions. In thinking about the specific position, you might begin with the following:

- Why is the position open?
- How long has the search been in progress and how long has the job been open? (If the position has been open for a long time, probe and find out why.)
- How many people have already been interviewed for the position? How many have met with the client? Are there any internal candidates? (With these questions, you are trying to establish who the competition is. If the client has interviewed a number of candidates already, probe deeper to try and find out why none of them has gotten—or accepted—the position.)
- What happened to the incumbent? Who were the last two people who held the position? Would it be possible to talk to them about the position? (If the incumbent was fired, don't ask this last question.)
- What are the job responsibilities? What kinds of projects would I be working on or involved with?
- To whom would I report in this position? Whom would I be managing or supervising? Who would be my key contacts both within and outside the company?
- What is the career path or tenure of the position?
- What is the turnover rate in the department? (This is to help you focus on possible problems in the department.)
- What is the company's reporting structure? Its corporate culture? Its political climate?
- What are the positive as well as the negative aspects to this position?

Ask as many questions as you deem important. Find out everything you want or need to know.

WHAT IMPRESSES THE RECRUITER

Recruiters like to think of themselves as tough customers. You have to be good to impress them, they tell you; they have an eye for matching the best talent with their clients, you know.

But there are several things that you can do that will particularly impress them:

Ask questions. "One of the most impressive things a candidate can do is ask questions—intelligent questions," says Allan Stern. It shows thought, preparation, and interest in addition to demonstrating the way your mind works.

Offer more than pat answers. The standard line, the well-worn phrase, the well-rehearsed answer—these will bore the recruiter as much as they bore you. Try to find a way to talk about yourself and your accomplishments in a framework that is both honest and fresh. For instance, "I know I'm supposed to say that I want to be a CEO one day, but quite frankly I see myself in a different role." Then explain what that role might be.

Follow up. After the initial interview, if both you and the recruiter are interested in pursuing the candidacy further, and you *still* have questions, don't be shy about asking to meet again, particularly to follow up on the "negatives" of the job. It's better for all concerned to get those questions answered before proceeding. The recruiter will be impressed with the seriousness of your approach.

Be human. You're a potential candidate, not an automaton. Since hiring decisions are based as much on that intangible thing known as "chemistry" as on hard qualifications, allow yourself to *be* yourself at the interview. Let your sense of humor show. Prepare answers beforehand for questions you expect, but don't recite them like a robot repeating a memorized response.

RED FLAGS FOR THE RECRUITER

Because recruiters are as much (if not more) in the business of screening candidates out as they are of screening them in, each one has his or her particular list of no-nos—the things that may impress, but hardly in the manner that you would like. Some of the warning signals they look for are obvious, others more subtle. Wave these red flags before a recruiter, and you might not be around long enough to find out what happens next:

You refuse to make eye contact. Refusing to meet the recruiter's eyes, hedging an answer, evading an issue—these are all signals that make the recruiter wonder: What is the candidate trying to hide? Why won't she answer me? Why is she so nervous? If she can't look me in the eye, how will she face a client or a superior? The straightforward candidate wins points; the evasive one loses them.

A divorce is in the works. "I believe in the premise that you make one major change at a time in your life, never two," Sydney Reynolds says, echoing the sentiments of other recruiters. Divorces are by definition stressful, they say; so are new jobs. Why tax yourself to the breaking point, in the process doing justice neither to your career nor to your personal life?

You're pregnant. You're planning to start a new job and then promptly go on maternity leave? You're going to tackle a challenging new position at work and simultaneously confront the challenge of being a new parent? Again, why stress yourself to the breaking point?

Further, since it's more common to look for a new job sometime *after* the maternity leave is over, most recruiters will suspect that the reason you're hunting now is because you have to leave. Even if that is the case, is it possible for you to work out a deal with your current company that would allow you to take a leave of absence that would extend until you find a new job *after* the baby's birth?

You would prefer not to answer. Yes, those personal questions may be illegal, but recruiters tend to ask them anyway, sometimes straightforwardly and without apology, more often with an informal, "Tell me about yourself." Regardless of the manner in which the question is asked, the recruiter will expect you to answer. "I respect their right not to discuss their personal life," Sydney Reynolds says. However, she would also probe more deeply to discover why the candidate prefers not to answer: "Is it a principle, or is it a rigidity of personality?"

You're too loquacious. If you know yourself to be a rambling talker, edit yourself. Your "opening remarks," discussed above, should last for no longer than ten minutes. If the recruiter asks you for three adjectives that your boss would use to describe your work style, provide three, not ten. However entertaining a conversationalist you might be, remember that this is a business—not a social—occasion. The recruiter is looking for a demonstration of your ability to *select* appropriate information; he does not want to hear all.

Make sure that what you do say is appropriate. "I'll say, 'Tell me something in the last six months that has caused stress,'" Chris Stevens says, "and they'll tell you that their boy friend left them or something to do with their husband. I'm looking for a job situation they had to handle!" If they'll tell me this, the recruiter thinks, what won't they tell anyone?

The person who talks nonstop raises another doubt in the recruiter's mind: When does she stop to listen?

You're a rolling stone. Have you jumped from company to company throughout your career? Are there several leaves of absence or other gaps between jobs? Why? Did you make a bad job choice or were you a victim of a corporate merger? Your reasons may be true and convincing. But if your pattern in the past raises questions, make sure you have compelling answers that would lead both the recruiter and the client to believe that you've changed your ways.

You bad-mouth your former company. "That sort of thing doesn't leave a good taste in anybody's mouth," even if the comments are justified, says Jean Boler of Handy Associates. When the recruiter asks why you changed jobs in the past, or why you might be looking to switch now, choose what you say carefully. If you're still bitter about a political difficulty or how you've been treated, perhaps you're not ready for an interview yet. Wait until you've cooled down and can present yourself as someone who can take things in stride rather than as an angry hothead.

You have too much personality—or not enough. It's one thing to make an impression, quite another to overwhelm the interviewer with your assertiveness or outrageous sense of humor. "Someone who is clearly abrasive and argumentative makes you wonder if there have been any people problems," Jean Boler comments. By contrast, the interviewee who blandly sits and answers patly will leave nothing behind at all, not even a memory.

You have no questions? If no questions at all have occurred to you, the recruiter will wonder how much time you have taken to think about the job, and, consequently, just how serious you are. Questions show interest: If you don't care enough to prepare for the interview, should the recruiter care enough to present you to the client?

You don't care about money? Really? "When I recruit prospective investment bankers and ask what are the things that attract them, if they don't list compensation among the top three or top five items at most, I know that person is lying," an investment banker says. No, money isn't everything, but it certainly is something; why not admit it?

You talk down to the recruiter. This is a sure way to insult one person you want to enlist as an ally. Find out the recruiter's level of expertise in your industry and respect it as you answer the questions. If the recruiter worked in your industry before changing careers, for instance, speak as an equal; don't condescend by explaining basics. If you're not certain just how much the recruiter knows, you can hedge by prefacing your remarks with the phrase, "As you know...."

You dress for failure. Even if you're meeting informally for a cup of coffee or a drink, dress for a business appointment. After all, this *is* a business appointment.

You take all the credit when it should be shared. Not only does this show a lack of team spirit and a tendency to be egotistical, it makes the recruiter question your credibility. Did you *really* plan and implement that new marketing concept all by yourself, without help from anyone else?

You say something that turns out not to be true. Never inflate your credentials or lie about your compensation. If you can't be trusted to tell the truth about yourself to the recruiter, why should an employer trust you with a senior-level position?

COURTSHIP MEETINGS THAT DON'T PAN OUT

"Thanks again for coming down to meet me today," the recruiter says. The proceedings have ended, you've shaken hands, and said good-bye. "I enjoyed our conversation," the headhunter continues, "but all things considered, I don't think this particular position is the best match for you. I'm sorry."

You're disappointed, but do not despair. If the position really was not right for you, the recruiter has just saved some time for all concerned.

Or perhaps you had come to the same conclusion yourself and gracefully said, "Perhaps another time."

If the recruiter disagrees with your assessment and wants you to consider the position further, he'll tell you so. But don't play hard to get when you really are interested; coyness is not highly regarded in the search business.

If you have established, however, that the recruiter is someone you would like to keep in touch with, make certain he knows that, too: "I hope you'll keep me in mind for a future search. If I can be of help, don't hesitate to call." Because headhunters can always use a good source, he won't hesitate at all.

Try to make your last impression as good as your first. Don't press for information that the recruiter may not be willing to give about why the match isn't right. You can express your disappointment—"I'm sorry this didn't work out, too"—but don't say good-bye on an angry or sour note. Do send a thank-you note, reinforcing your willingness to help when future searches arise.

Do you want feedback on your interview performance? You may ask for it, but don't expect any. Again, recruiters aren't career counselors, and since their loyalty is to their clients rather than their candidates, they have little to gain by giving you advice. So don't expect more than a vague, noncommittal response, such as, "The chemistry isn't right," or "They're looking for someone with a more technical background." If you hear more than that, you're hearing more than most.

Finally, don't expect to hear from the recruiter again until another search comes up. In the meantime, follow up with an updated resume about once a year. Send any articles you have written or newspaper clippings that report your latest accomplishment. When that next search does arise, the recruiter will have your file at hand and your phone number in his Rolodex.

BEFORE YOU MEET THE CLIENT

"So think about it," the recruiter says at the end of your first meeting. "You'll hear from me soon." And when you do, the recruiter says, "The client would like to meet you."

You're one step closer, but there's still far to go. What's next?

First, don't feel so flattered by the fact that *they're* pursuing you that you decide you need do little more than passively wait for an offer. Your nonchalance will be perceived by recruiter and client alike as lack of interest.

By contrast, "One of the most impressive things you can do is go into that meeting prepared," Dee Soder says.

Even before meeting the client, Allan Stern advises, don't be afraid to ask *the recruiter* for a follow-up meeting to discuss the position's drawbacks. "Often candidates can be enticed by what they've heard, but may be scared to ask for more information because they think the consultant might eliminate them if they say, 'I want to talk about the problem areas. I have these questions.' But that makes a positive, rather than a negative impression."

Ask specific questions about all the different aspects that concern you: What are the management styles of the people for and with whom you would be working? What is the company's position in the market relative to the company you work for now? What are the prospects for your future there, as opposed to where you are now? Why is this job open? Did someone leave—and if so, why? Has the company created a new position, and if so, why? How have other women done at the company? Can women succeed there?

Before meeting the client, get as much information as you can about the company and the executives who work there. The recruiter can be expected to provide you with some information and even prep you about an executive's demeanor: "He can be intimidating, but don't let that scowl scare you." Or, "He has a deadpan expression that can be misleading; you think he's not responding to what you're saying, but he's taking it all in."

Although such hints are helpful, remember that the recruiter represents the client. Even if he knew *all* the drawbacks, would he present them to you in the worst possible light, or in the best?

With this in mind, regard the information that the recruiter provides as only the introductory chapter to your own research. The rest is up to you. How well you do your homework may be taken not only as an indication of how serious you are about the position, but how thoroughly you would prepare for any important business meeting. This is an important meeting, after all. It could affect your future.

Ask for the company's annual report and go to the library to look for whatever proxy statements or articles about the company you can find. Check the *Reader's Guide to Periodical Literature* and the *New York Times Index* for any major articles that may have appeared about the company. If you want to be even more thorough, look at *How to Find Information About Companies,* published by Washington Researchers, a book that will tell you, step by step, how to go about gathering information from the government, the courts, trade associations, data bases, and so on.

Do you know someone who works for the company? Call and find out what it's like to work there: What's the political atmosphere? The corporate culture? Is everyone a workaholic, or are they nine-to-fivers?

Whom else do you know who might know something? Call colleagues, acquaintances from your professional association, or friends who work at other companies, but be smart about whom you choose to contact. You don't want to phone someone who might also be a candidate for the job, nor do you want to call jealous souls who might misconstrue your desire for information as a wish to show off. Make sure you can count on the people you call to keep the information confidential and not indiscreetly spill the beans.

Play the investigative reporter on your own behalf. Don't wait until a cover story in *Forbes* or *Business Week* hits you with all the terrible facts that you *should* have known before accepting the job—but that you did not take the time to uncover yourself.

MEETING THE CLIENT

Before you meet the client, the recruiter will have "presented" you to him, describing you over the telephone or in writing, or both. The recruiter may have sent your original resume or one written by the recruiter which emphasizes your strengths for the position. The recruiter's cover letter will reiterate those strengths and may also point out problem areas or facets that the client might wish to explore further when he meets you.

Now that the client knows about you, and you have found out about him, it is time for you to meet.

Most likely, you'll meet alone; there will be no recruiter there to chaperone you. Recruiters only occasionally sit in on this meeting. They'll hear about it later from both the client and from you.

The same rules apply to this interview that apply to any interview. In meeting you, however, the client will expect to find not only a highly qualified candidate who satisfies the job's requirements, but a highly motivated individual who has come prepared for the interview. After all, the client hired the recruiter precisely to find that kind of candidate.

The client may ask background questions similar to those the recruiter asked. But the client may be far more specific in his questions, asking how you would respond to particular situations, problems, or conflicts.

You, too, will ask the client some of the same questions you asked the recruiter. But based on your further research, these questions will also be more specific.

Here are some questions you might ask:

How do you define the job? You'll want to know the specifics of the job, from budget numbers to numbers of people managed. Make sure you know exactly what the responsibilities of the job are and what you're being hired to do. "I know of a person who was going to take a job selling a financial product, but didn't understand what the product was," Dee Soder says. "Well, you'd better understand what the product is because you're going to be out there selling it! And it may be unsellable."

How would you define a successful manager in this position? If the position is a new one, this question might help your interviewer to think through who he is looking for as much as it helps you to understand what skills the job will require. If you are filling a position that already exists, ask why the position is open and about the prior incumbents in this position. What did the previous person do well? What would your interviewer have liked him to have done differently? Is it possible to arrange to talk with that person? (If the person was fired, it probably would not be.)

What are the objectives of the position? There are formal and informal objectives to every job, Soder points out, and sometimes they won't be the same at all. For instance, a job's stated, or formal, objective may be to produce x-number of widgets; but the job's unstated, informal objective may be to bring a fresh perspective to the division, or to encourage more cooperation between departments. And that unstated objective, Soder asserts, may count as much or more as the stated one.

So when you ask about the job's "formal" objectives, listen carefully. The way the client words his answer may provide the underlying message that will tell you what the job's other, unstated objectives really are.

Who are the people I would be working with in this position? Ask for descriptions of the people you'll be working for and with. If the job is a management position, how many people will you be managing, and what are they like? What are the management styles of the people with whom you would have substantial interactions on the job? Who would be your "key contacts" in your department, in other departments in the company, and outside the company? How does your style mesh with theirs?

What is the management structure of the company? Of the department? Of the position? What does the company's organizational chart look like? With what divisions would you be working? Can you meet people in those divisions? Have there been any difficulties in the working relationship between divisions? The answers will tell you a good bit about the company's team spirit or lack of it.

What has been the turnover rate in the department? Is it a stable department? Or is it one that has problems keeping people? If so, why? What have the problems been in the past? Is the department *too* stable? One of the unstated reasons the client wishes to hire someone new may be to bring a fresh perspective to the department.

Who have been the successful executives in this company and what has enabled them to be so successful? With this question, you are trying to discover several things. First, you're attempting to find out how people progress in their careers at this company. Next, you're trying to ascertain who has done well coming from outside the company and what made for that person's success. Finally, you want to know who from outside did not succeed and why.

What is the career progression of this position? You'll want to find out where this position may lead and compare the opportunities presented here to the opportunities in store for you at your current position. What happened to the prior incumbents in the position may give you additional clues.

Would it be possible for me to talk to people at different levels in the company? Some companies routinely ask employees at different job levels to interview a job candidate in order to make sure that the fit is right. The company wants to find out: How does he strike top management to whom he will report, as compared to potential peers and subordinates? From the candidate's point of view, such meetings can provide a vivid portrait of the company as a whole—what kind of sense of humor people favor, what sports are popular, what staff members think, talk, and care about. Are those the same subjects that concern you? Can you see yourself fitting into this group portrait, too?

How do people work in this company? How do people dress? Do people come in early or late? How do people pace their days? Will you be expected to spend your weekends playing golf with clients? What if you hate golf? If the company places a high value on community projects, with what volunteer work would you involve yourself? Asking these questions is another way of finding out about the company's corporate culture.

Are any changes anticipated in the company over the next

year? The next five years? The next decade? Dee Soder says
that this question will demonstrate your need to know press-
ing information about the present, as well as your interest in
making a long-term commitment.

You may notice that none of these questions pertained to
money. Well, as stated earlier, long before meeting the client,
you should have established the general salary range with the
recruiter. Further, for higher-level positions in particular, what
you want to focus on now is the position and how well you
and the company fit each other. As more than one executive
recruiter says, "The money will take care of itself later."

However, if, in talking to the client, you sense a real discrepancy between the kind of position that the recruiter described
to you as opposed to the types of responsibility the client is
now focusing on, tactfully bring up the subject. Say, "I'm sorry,
but I'm a little confused here. From what I understood, the
position would be another managerial level above this."

And if you're still uncertain, ask for specifics: "I appreciate
your taking the time to flesh out the position for me here. Can
you give me an idea of your compensation range and your typical benefits package?"

Pay close attention to the way your interviewer frames his
answers. If the company stresses team spirit, why does the
interviewer keep saying "I," never "we"? Whenever you mention a certain subject, do you notice a sudden hedging, stam-
mering, or averting of the eyes? Is there something more there?
If you spot such a discrepancy, dig to find out more. Talk to
your friends in the professional association and track down
people who currently work for the company or who worked
there in the past. Tell the recruiter your concerns. Check the
different stories and come to your own conclusions.

If both you and the client company remain interested in
each other, subsequent meetings will be arranged. Even if an
offer is made on the spot and you're tempted to say yes, make
certain to meet again, anyway. Counselors and recruiters advise against making any major job change without at least two
substantive meetings with people from the company. Would

you buy a house without first thoroughly examining the premises and checking the financing? If the company urges you to make a decision on the spot, find out why: something could be seriously wrong.

At subsequent meetings, you'll have a chance to explore any more questions you might have. Of course, the company's executives will also have many questions for you, and on occasion, some very odd tests. One successful candidate relates that before being presented with a formal job offer, she was invited to a breakfast meeting with the head of the organization in order to test her table manners!

RECRUITER AS GO-BETWEEN

The conversations are between you and the client now, so where does the recruiter fit into all this? He is a go-between, buffer, and middleman, part counselor and part confidant.

Expect to speak to him shortly after your meeting with the client. He may call you at home or ask that you call him. He will probably want to get your feedback on the meeting before he speaks to the client. In discussing your meeting, be straightforward but discreet; the recruiter does work for the client, and it is a small world.

Tell him your thoughts: Did the meeting go well? Are you still interested? If so, how interested? Are you still uncertain? What are your areas of concern? All things considered, are you inclined to drop out of consideration?

If there are questions or discrepancies, ask about them: "I thought the job had to do with developing a new product altogether, rather than revamping an older one." Or, "I thought we were talking about $100,000, but he seems to be talking about no more than $75,000."

If the chemistry doesn't seem right to you, say that, too. If you do decide at this point that the position is not for you, speak now to avoid dragging out the process. Are you considering using an offer as a bargaining point for your current company? Neither the recruiter nor the company will appreciate being used in this way, and your current company might not go for such tactics, either. Similarly, if at any other point along the way you decide to rule yourself out, tell the recruiter.

If you want to write the client a thank-you note or send additional material—an article you mentioned in your discussion or a speech you wrote—check with the recruiter first. Different recruiters work differently, and his response may also depend on his relationship with the client, the nature of the position, and how the interview went. Whatever the reason, your recruiter may not like your contacting the client directly or without informing him first.

Ask the recruiter about what comes next. Will he call you after he speaks to the client? When can you expect that call? Should you call the recruiter, and if so, when? Set a timetable so that you will not appear either to be nagging the recruiter (calling more than once a week is considered badgering) or so lacking in interest that you cannot find the time to phone him.

Perhaps the most tactful thing to do is ask if you can periodically check with the recruiter's secretary to see if the search is continuing and if you're still a candidate. From the recruiter's point of view, that will be one less phone call he has to make, and you will have access to the information you want.

But it's also the recruiter's job to keep good candidates interested. If the search drags on but you continue to be in contention, you should also expect to hear from him, saying, "You're one of three finalists." Or, "The client hasn't made up his mind yet; this might take a while." Or even, "You're not number one or two, but you also haven't been ruled out yet."

LAST IMPRESSIONS

What if it turns out that you no longer are in the running? Or what if you decide to take yourself out of the race? What is the etiquette for closing the chase?

Many recruiters admittedly dislike making that phone call

saying, "Sorry, it just didn't work out." Although a good recruiter will always pave the way for future interactions by
being courteous now, some may just let you fade away rather
than tell you "no" directly.

But whether the recruiter calls you to tell you the news directly or you have to track him down to get the answer, the
way in which you handle this final conversation will help determine the course of your future dealings with each other.

Angry outbursts, hostile comments, or other fits of pique
clearly won't encourage the recruiter to call you again, either
as a source or a candidate. It won't win you any points to burst
out, as one candidate did, "Well, I'm very disappointed because I really think this company needs me desperately!"

The same recruiter at whom this outburst was directed recalls another candidate who expressed disappointment, but in
a very different way. Upon learning that, after protracted interviews and negotiations, the expected job offer was not forthcoming, the candidate nonetheless wrote a dignified thank-
you letter, carefully not placing blame on any party, and offering any assistance he might be able to provide in future
searches. Impressed by his attitude, the recruiter has made a
point of keeping in touch with him.

So when the recruiter's answer is no, stay cool. Control your
emotions. Offer your services as a source. Chances are you'll
hear from the recruiter again.

Similarly, if you decide to take yourself out of consideration,
do so graciously, thanking both the recruiter and the client for
the opportunity to be considered. When your paths cross
again, there will be no unfinished business to consider.

REFERENCE CHECKS

Most recruiters won't begin formally checking references
until an offer is about to be, or already has been, made.
However, before you're even presented to a client, many recruiters will do what they call a preliminary reference check:

That means they already will have gotten a feel for who you are from their sourcing calls and the comments made by the people who recommended you. Many firms also will verify education or industry credentials. If a discrepancy appears, don't bet on your candidacy for the job going any further. "If someone says they have a Ph.D., but they're really ABD [all-but-dissertation], that's a serious question," Jeanne Marie Gilbert says. "If they're good enough, we *might* still present them, but we would tell the client." And that, she says, happens "only *very* occasionally."

Reference checking at any stage is a delicate matter, recruiters agree. On the one hand, they don't want to arouse suspicion and inadvertently endanger the candidate's current position. On the other, they want to make certain that this is the right person for the position, in terms of both qualifications and personality.

To this end, the recruiter will ask for three or four references. *Always alert your references that they may be receiving a call.* Describe the position, say why you think it's a good move for you, and explain how you see it fitting into your career as a whole. Don't let the recruiter take your references by surprise. Just think how it sounds: "Oh, I didn't even know Jean was looking for a job!" The better prepared the person is, the better a reference you'll receive.

Reference checks have become harder to perform in recent years; companies are afraid former employees will sue them if they think a bad reference has prevented them from getting another job. But recruiters, being savvy networkers, will call different contacts until they get the verification they need.

If your job situation is particularly sensitive, alert the recruiter at the start. "Candidates can insist that no one in their current company be contacted until they give the word," Alice Early points out. "There are times when we have gone to the very end, with a tentative acceptance of the offer, before checking the references."

WHEN AN OFFER IS MADE: WEIGHING THE DECISION

To accept or not to accept. The offer may come from the recruiter or from the client himself. Regardless of who presents it, what matters now is your decision. In weighing the job offer, consider your past and your future in relation to the present.

Where have you been? Look at your career as a whole. Is this only your first or second job change since you began your career, or is it your fifth in as many years? Recruiters agree that too many changes will raise questions, but so does staying in one place forever. "The company wants to make sure, by the time you're in your forties, that you've worked for several companies and have an idea of different corporate cultures," Allan Stern comments. Is this a move that will show you to be someone who is flexible and can work in different environments—or will it appear to be more proof that you just don't like to stay put?

"Use mobility, but use it selectively," Ann Powers Kern of Korn/Ferry, advises. "Success is still based on a solid record of sustained achievement."

Where are you now? Evaluate your current position. What do you like about it? What drives you crazy? What is the career path before you if you stay put? Is that the path you prefer, or only the path of least resistance?

How does your current position compare to your prospective one? What are the things that attract you to the new position? Do they outweigh the things you value at your current position? What about the negative aspects of the new position? Make sure you're not trading in one problematic situation for another. What career path do you foresee at your new company? What future opportunities does the new job offer that your current one does not? What are the opportunities that your current job may offer that this one does not?

Where are you going? Ideally, where would you like your career path to take you? Perhaps, considering your current situation, it really is time to move on. In that case, is this the opportunity that *should* make you move? Would it really bring you closer to your larger goals?

How good a fit is it? How well do your values mesh with those of the company? Is the corporate culture one that is amenable to you? One that is amenable to women? How does this fit compare to the fit you have now? What are the risks if it turns out to be an uncomfortable fit? Go over all your research about the company. Replay the answers to the questions you asked in your meetings and interviews. If you still have questions, ask them. Investigate the position and the company as thoroughly as possible before making your decision.

Is an itch to move reason enough to move? Maybe it's not the best move, you conclude, but it is time to move. Should you accept the position on that basis alone? "More often than not, people know that they're in the wrong position, but they're too lazy to make a change," Allan Stern comments. But if you change jobs only because the opportunity is there, don't expect to be any happier at this position than you were at the last.

What about the money? A substantial increase in salary may be a tempting reason to move, but don't let it be the only reason, particularly if you have serious reservations about the position itself. Similarly, if the opportunity offers everything you're looking for, but the compensation package is less than your current salary, should that be the determining factor in saying no?

"The main reason to move should be all the other things— the opportunity, the company, the culture—all the soft things," Stern says. "The last thing one should consider is the money."

Nonetheless, "You also shouldn't move unless you're getting a sizable increase in pay—in the 30 percent range, especially if you're relocating—because you're taking a greater risk," comments Ann Powers Kern of Korn/Ferry. "If you cannot negotiate a higher recognition level in the new job in terms of both responsibility and dollars, then your chances for success are diminished."

Allan Stern uses the same logic, but comes up with different figures, commenting, "In terms of compensation, there aren't any rules. I've seen people move at the same level, for 10 percent higher, for 100 percent higher." However, he says, at a time when an annual salary increase averages 5 to 7 percent, "If someone can increase compensation by 15 percent, that's not bad."

But whether you move for a 15 or a 30 percent salary increase, these recruiters agree, your decision should rest less on money than on the risks involved and the opportunities you foresee.

What if you still have more questions? Don't hesitate to ask your questions. It's in everyone's interest to make sure your reservations are aired and your problems resolved. However, if, after repeated meetings and offers and counter-offers, you still can't come to a conclusion, the recruiter and client will begin to wonder why not. Does your indecision show that you're not ready to make a move, after all? Are you *always* this indecisive? What would you do in a difficult business situation? Other questions might be raised as well: Are you just playing hard to get? Or are you maneuvering as part of a more complicated political game?

Be straightforward with the recruiter, the client, and yourself. Reflect on the reasons for your inability to decide and discuss your doubts or apprehensions with the recruiter.

Do you feel the recruiter is rushing your decision? If the job isn't quite right, don't count on the recruiter to tell you *not* to take the job. Remember that some recruiters just want to close the deal and move on to the next search—and the next fee.

Good recruiters, however, will give you honest advice: "I think you'll be great at this—except you'll hate it," Dee Soder remembers telling a candidate once. Another recruiter recalls pulling a candidate out of a search just before the final offer was to be made upon realizing that, because their personalities and work styles were so different, the client and candidate could not possibly work well together. When given, this kind of advice is not offered for humanitarian reasons alone: The longer you remain and the more successful you prove at the job, the better the recruiter will look, too. Regardless of what the recruiter tells you, never forget that the person who has the biggest stake in this decision is you.

NEGOTIATING THE DEAL: WHOM DOES THE RECRUITER REPRESENT?

The offer is on the table. The prospect is tempting, you're inclined to say yes, but there are a few wrinkles you'd still like to iron out—about compensation and incentives, and about the perks you had in your last position which you'd like to have in this one, too.

How do you negotiate the best deal possible? Furthermore, *who* will do the negotiating? If the recruiter acts as the go-between—and the recruiter almost always does—whom will he be representing? The client—*his* client—or you?

Even without this conflict of interest over whom the recruiter is *really* representing in the negotiations, some candidates chafe at the thought of a go-between. They feel that anything the recruiter can negotiate, they can negotiate better themselves.

Recruiters admit that there *is* an apparent conflict of interest, but they also argue that candidates should trust the recruiter to handle the negotiations. "In many cases they're going to get a better deal by dealing through us," Allan Stern asserts, "because the client, in many cases, is much more insulated and doesn't know what it would take to make the candidate move and, as a result, might offer less money than we would." However, Stern acknowledges, if the client wants to offer you more than the going rate, the recruiter would also advise the client to offer you less money.

Yet there is a most compelling reason for using the recruiter in the negotiations: Should any difficulties or disagreements occur, he will act as your buffer, protecting you from any mis-understandings or bad feelings that might arise as a result of the negotiations.

In smaller companies, in particular, the head of the company himself may be involved in the negotiations, Stern points out. "You want to start off on the right foot. You don't want to have bad feelings as a result of haggling over a few thousand dollars. We want to preserve the good feelings.... We're in the middle, so everyone can blame us."

HOW TO NEGOTIATE THE BEST DEAL

Recruiters and career counselors agree that there are several steps to negotiating the best deal:

Step one: Be honest and thorough with the recruiter. Even before an offer is made, the recruiter will want to review with you your current compensation package and compensation history. Be straightforward; the recruiter will find out in his reference checks if you're inflating any of the figures.

Be certain to tell the recruiter exactly how your compensation is structured. If this year's bonus was lower than last year's, not because of your individual performance but because the company as a whole did poorly, state that clearly. Similarly, if you are coming up for a raise within six months, tell him what the expected increase will be. And don't forget to mention any and all benefits or perks your current position carries with it: expense account, company car, etc. Usually, the recruiter will give you a general idea of what the compensation package will be before the actual figures are presented. The more thoroughly you discuss everything beforehand, the fewer surprises you'll have once the formal offer is presented.

Step two: Do your research. Once again, it's time for some homework. What are the standard compensation levels within the industry? What are the standards within this particular company? Business and trade journals often publish such information, so go to the library or call the magazine's editorial office. Trade associations frequently gather this information, too; find out if yours does.

"Find out what people are being paid in comparable branches, in comparable firms, with comparable educational backgrounds," says Camille Lavington, a communications and career consultant in New York City. "This is why you belong to different groups, why you know different recruiters, why you serve on committees—so you can get the inside information." With this information in hand, you'll be able to judge if your offer is reasonable and ready to gauge how much leeway you will have in your negotiations.

Step three: Review your current compensation. Go over *all* the pieces of your compensation package once again. Did you forget to discuss anything with the recruiter beforehand? Are there any important areas that you've missed that you should go over *before* the offer is made?

How does the probable offer the recruiter described compare with what you can expect if you stay? What happens when you weigh the two against each other, point by point? Will the differences be enough to persuade you to move?

Step four: Know what you want. What *would* it take to persuade you to move? "Know what you want," Nella Barkley counsels, and by that she means "a lot more than dollars and cents." For example, in terms of compensation, perhaps stock options, bonus arrangements, or performance appraisals linked to raises matter to you. Or it's not the compensation, so much as things like title, support staff, or the particular office you'd be given that concern you. Or perhaps you would like to request a day to work at home each week, or want to iron out provisions concerning child care. As long as the requests are reasonable and within the realm of possibility at the company, you can make them. But be prepared to ask now, when you *can* negotiate. At the moment you have the upper hand; the company wants you and will be inclined to give you at least some of what you want. After you actually start the job, it will be too late to ask.

Step five: Order your priorities. You know what you want

ideally. But what if some items—a title, a company car, the day to work at home each week—simply cannot be arranged? What items are negotiable? What items are not? How flexible are you willing to be? Are there substitutions you would accept? If you know what you want, you can order your priorities. For example, you can live without the title or the company car, but you can't live without good support staff. Or you would be willing to sacrifice something else in order to get that one day a week to work at home. Remember that in order to get something, you usually have to give up something else. So know what you want to get, and what you can give up.

Step six: Rehearse your presentation: The offer has been made, and you've asked for time to think it over. It sounds tempting, but there are questions you'd like to go over. How do you present your requests?

Go over your priorities once again and rehearse what you want to say beforehand: "I have a few questions about the compensation level. Could we go over the structure of the incentives plan? I'd prefer a performance review at six months rather than nine. I understand it's your policy not to give people that day to work at home, but I wonder if there's some other way we could arrange that."

Be aware that there is a particular order in which to negotiate. "Get money out of the way first," Nella Barkley says, "then the total compensation package, with pension plans and their structure. Then you go to your other working conditions."

In stating your points, don't be hostile, curt, or defensive. "Present these requests easily, conversationally, not like bullets being fired out," Barkley advises. "Say, 'Well, tell me what the office arrangement is.' That's your opportunity to say, 'An office like this would not be good for me because of the commotion that is going on in the corridor; would it be possible to find something still accessible, but a little more removed?' But if you get into that office and then try to get those things done, you'll have much more trouble."

Whatever requests you make, Barkley says, "Be sure that

what you are presenting is not only an advantage for you, but that it is also an advantage for them, and that they will get more out of you as a result." The point, after all, is to try to get the best you can from the company, without seeming to get the best *of* the company. If that happens, Barkley warns, "They will get you in the long run." And so in winning your points, beware of also stirring up feelings of resentment in your prospective boss or in future colleagues who may not have done as well in *their* negotiations.

Step seven: *Retain your composure.* Even the most composed executives sometimes gulp when they face negotiations, recruiters say. But you should not swallow an offer that isn't right. Even the company does not want you to feel taken advantage of; smart bosses know that the executive who is disgruntled from the start is less likely to put forth the best effort. And a poor performance on the job won't do much for your reputation, either.

"If the figure is not high enough, you can negotiate for other perks," Camille Lavington advises. "And you can ask for a period of time before you're eligible for those perks—'If I go in at this level, can we agree that you will review me in six months?'—and set another benchmark."

Don't be afraid to raise questions about points that don't sit quite right with you or that you don't understand. "Some people are afraid to argue because they fear that the deal will collapse," Lavington says. "Or they want to separate themselves from the 'people who do that kind of thing.' The executive recruiter is a big asset to you in this because that's your middleman, your broker," and any arguments that arise will be with him, not your future boss.

Be flexible in the negotiations, but be assertive. Remember that you have a far better bargaining position now than you will have later. If you feel uncomfortable with the numbers, or you think that a benefit that should be there is missing, speak up in a calm, reasonable voice. If the recruiter says that the request is not reasonable, go back and look at your research. Is it? Don't forget that in order to win one point, it's often necessary to concede another. But if the recruiter tries to rush you to a decision, remember that it's your career, not his.

As you go through the negotiations, strike a balance between being tough yet conciliatory. Be prepared to accept compromise; you want the client company to feel that you're willing to be flexible, that you can give as well as take. But you can only come to comfortable compromises if you know what you want, and if you know how to ask.

Step eight: Remember that this is not a one-step process. "Recognize that this can be a three- or four-step process," Camille Lavington says. Ask for time to think things through. If you're still not satisfied, perhaps you need another step in the negotiations. "Never give a direct answer immediately when the offer is made," she says. "Ask for time to think about and digest the offer." And remember that "It's a barter point at all levels." That also means knowing what you can give up in order to get what you want.

Step nine: Is this the deal you want? There will always be compromises—that's what the give and take of negotiations are all about. And so what it all comes down to in the end, Alice Early says, is fairness: "What the candidate wants to know is, 'This is the best offer that the client can make.' Everyone wants to feel they have come to a fair resolution. It does nobody any good to have one party feel squeezed or ill-used." Bad feelings on either side can come back to haunt you later. In the end, both you and the company should feel that the deal you've worked out is an attractive one.

Nonetheless, make certain that this is not only a deal that you *can* live with but one that you *want* to live with. "You're establishing your self-worth at the outset," Lavington advises. "Your future raises and opportunities are based on that beginning. Many people think that they can turn things around later, after they've proven themselves. They think that people will give what they want and what they deserve. But it doesn't work that way."

Step ten: Come to a decision. Weigh everything once again.

List all the pluses and minuses of both positions. Are you satisfied that this is the best deal? Recruiters and counselors alike point out that there is no such thing as a perfect job or a perfect deal. But are you making the *right* decision? Take time to think through all your options; talk to your family and to your colleagues. Does anything still rankle? Why? Is that enough to make you say no? Are you focusing on a single negative aspect at the expense of the larger picture? Look at this decision within the context of your career and your life as a whole. If the fit is right, then you have your answer.

Step eleven: Dealing with a counter-offer. Sometimes, after you've accepted the new position and you've given notice, there will be a counter-offer from your current company. Your decision to leave was genuine, but now you're torn. Weigh everything once again and decide, all things considered, which would be the best move for you. If you decide to remain at your present job, be gracious, and call or write both the recruiter and the company executives involved.

Of course, this assumes that you weren't setting this all up in order to improve your current position. Be on the up-and-up with the recruiter and don't play games, Ann Powers Kern of Korn/Ferry warns. "Because if you aren't [being straightforward], and the recruiter learns that, then you won't be trusted the next time." Further, if your current company feels used, they won't like it, either.

SHOULD YOU ASK FOR AN EMPLOYMENT AGREEMENT?

"I think that a company today should be prepared to make whatever offer they're making verbally in writing," Allan Stern says. "That's number one. And number two is, a contract comes down to one thing: How much do I get paid if I get fired?"

This is an important point: With so many takeovers and acquisitions occurring, can you be certain that the person who hires you today will be there next year, or when the company is bought? Can you be certain, in any case, that the boss who hires you today will be there a year from now?

In general, formal contracts, drawn up by a lawyer, are reserved for executives at the highest, most responsible positions within a company. Even if you have not reached that exalted level, however, you may ask for an offering letter that would state the compensation, bonus arrangements and stock options, relocation plan, any other conditions or special perks, and what you will receive if you are fired.

Sometimes the company will allow you to draft this letter yourself. Or they will ask you to write a letter addressed to your employer, which the employer will then countersign. Give him a copy for his files, then keep the original for yourself—

And prepare to begin your new job.

STAYING IN THE HEADHUNTER'S DATA BANK

You've shaken hands and closed the deal. You've been successfully placed in your new job, so what happens to your relationship with the recruiter now? "A good search consultant is going to keep in touch with the people he has placed," Allan Stern says. "You are automatically on his list to check on." You can count on the recruiter to stay in touch with you.

Beyond a humanistic interest in how well you do, there's one obvious reason for recruiters to stay in touch with their placements: You may be in a position to hire other executives —and to hire recruiters to find them.

But what if you didn't get *this* job?

Follow up. "Everybody should make up their resume once a year," Stern advises, "because what you're doing is putting down accomplishments for the last year. And if on New Year's Eve you can't think of any accomplishments, then it's time to make a move.

"At the same time, it's important because if after fifteen

years in business you're asked to make up a resume, you're not going to remember your accomplishments. So it becomes almost like a diary or a log."

So send your updated resume annually. Remain visible. Act the good source. Do the best job you can. Is it magic? The recruiters will be in touch.

6

CAREFUL OR YOU MIGHT GET SCALPED: WARNINGS AND CAVEATS AND SOME FINAL WORDS

As the previous chapters have shown, recruiters can do much to help executives in their careers. Yet you have also seen that there are various traps and pitfalls that may lie in wait along the way. Although I've covered these points in detail elsewhere in the book, they warrant repetition here.

Here's a final checklist:

- Make sure the recruiter is reputable.
- Guard your confidentiality.
- Never let a recruiter talk you into a job you don't want to take.
- Keep the recruiter's role in perspective.

RECRUITERS TO BE WARY OF

How can you tell if the recruiter is not on the up-and-up? Here are some characters to watch out for:

- The recruiter who sings you a song about offering you the best professional opportunity you ever heard.
- The recruiter who asks you for a fee for his services.
- The recruiter who describes one job—and then sends you on an interview for a different kind of position altogether.

- The recruiter who puts undue pressure on you to interview for, or accept, a position you know just isn't right for you.
- The recruiter who offers you money under the table for accepting a position.

If a recruiter does any of these things, beware. If you have serious doubts or questions about the recruiter, call one of the executive recruiter trade associations or the Better Business Bureau.

GUARDING YOUR CONFIDENTIALITY

If your current position is not in any danger, you want to make doubly certain that the recruiter respects your need for confidentiality. To help ensure it:

- Ascertain whether or not the recruiter actually has a position for you. Does he want to speak to you about a particular position? Or does he see you as just another resume to market with the rest of his wares?
- Never send your resume to a recruiter you haven't met, of whose reputation you are uncertain, or whom you have not checked on.
- Make sure that the recruiter agrees to consult you *before* submitting your name or your resume to a client. The last thing you want is your resume to turn up "accidentally" at a subsidiary of your current firm—or on your boss's desk.
- Never work with a recruiter whose professionalism you question.

TO ANSWER OR NOT TO ANSWER

"I know it's illegal, but I'm asking anyway," the recruiter tells you.
   What do you say?

Refusing to answer may be the principled thing to do. But the truth of the matter is that many recruiters will rule you out from consideration if you do refuse. (Then again, you might say, do you even want to work with a recruiter or prospective employer who would base a decision on this information?)

Usually, however, the questions will be phrased more subtly. The recruiter will say, "Tell me about your lifestyle," or "What's important to you?" or simply, "Tell me about yourself."

It may be illegal to *ask* the questions; but there is no law against your volunteering the information yourself. And since most recruiters do want this information, the practical job seeker is advised to prepare a discreet answer beforehand that tells enough—but does not tell too much.

OTHER TRICK QUESTIONS

Occasionally, a recruiter will put a candidate through a high-stress interview. You'll know it when you come across it. He'll bait you, insult you, belittle you. And you, a well-mannered person unaccustomed to such behavior, will wonder what to do. Do you sit there and politely take it, or tell the churl to shut up? Your response will determine whether or not you "pass" his interview exam.

For what the recruiter is doing in such an interview is testing your assertiveness and aggressiveness. He's waiting for you to show him your stuff. But though interviewers who use this tactic justify it on the grounds that it helps them to screen people for high-stress positions, one wonders how effectively this kind of showmanship really mirrors the stress the job itself will bring. Nonetheless, as long as some recruiters still believe it will, be prepared.

And how do you pass the high-stress interview? By keeping cool and answering the questions as best you can. In some cases, the interviewer will be trying to simulate the kind of high-stress environment that you would encounter on the job itself. Keeping that in mind, retain your dignity and respond to the questions. If, however, the interviewer's behavior goes beyond a plausible simulation and begins to border on abuse, you might ask—as tactfully or graciously as the situation allows—is this the wrong time to discuss the issues? If you must leave, do so with your dignity intact.

IS THIS A JOB OFFER YOU CAN REFUSE?

"Well, it's not exactly what you want," the recruiter says, "but it is a step up, and it is a great company. So why don't you try it for a while, until the next job comes along?"

If your answer is no, be firm. What's at stake for the recruiter is a fee; what's at stake for you is your career.

KEEPING THE HEADHUNTER IN PERSPECTIVE

"A recruiter is far from the solution to all the world's problems," Thomas Ogdon admits. "In many cases, he's going to be of very limited value to a specific person in thinking through career changes which can be very difficult, and which need to be thought through oneself. The recruiter's going to be stingy with his time. He's not going to give away potential client contacts."

Further, as legal recruiter Carol Kanarek points out, "Maybe five percent of the jobs for lawyers go through search firms." To look for a legal position *only* through a recruiter would limit you considerably. Similar warnings would apply to other industries. Allan Stern estimates that perhaps no more than 10 to 15 percent of all executive positions are filled through recruiters. Although these numbers represent an important chunk of the positions available, please don't count on the recruiter alone to find a job for you. Use the recruiter as one resource among others.

Recruiters, in sum, can be an excellent resource; that has been the subject of this book. Put their role in perspective, learn how to work with them, and they will provide a valuable service. They can help place you in positions you would not have known of otherwise. They can provide introductions to companies to which you would not have otherwise had access. They can be one of your best resources when you find yourself ready to make a career move. And sometimes, just by calling or courting you, they can serve as the catalyst that forces you to think seriously about your career. In the end, however, the role they play depends on you. Place that role in the larger perspective of your career as a whole. This is your career, after all. Manage it well.

7

YOUR DATA BANK: LISTINGS AND RESOURCES

Because there are literally thousands of executive-search firms in the United States today, the following list was designed as a starting point only. It will give you a good idea of what exists, but it is no more than an introduction to the vast universe of firms engaged in screening job seekers' resumes and competing for business with client companies.

In using this list, remember that in the same way that your resume changes or needs updating yearly, so do lists of executive recruiters. New firms start up, and older firms merge. An address or phone number may change, or a firm may change its emphasis from one field to another, or switch from contingency to retainer. The partner or associate you knew from one of the large firms may decide to break away to form a smaller firm of his or her own.

For these reasons, you should call before writing to a particular firm. Get the name of the person who specializes in your particular field of expertise. Ask for brochures and other information.

An appendix and annotated bibliography at the conclusion of this section will provide suggestions for further resources.

EXECUTIVE-RECRUITING FIRMS

Kenneth J. Cole, publisher of the *Recruiting & Search Report*, very graciously provided the information for the following listings. His extensive listings may be ordered directly from him at P. O. Box 9433, Panama City Beach, Florida 32407 (Telephone: 904-235-3733). He publishes about 60 individual directories, each of which concentrates on a specific industry, function, area of the country, or type of firm. They cost nine dollars each, and a minimum of three must be ordered. He has offered to send the current "Superior Campaigning Executive & Professional Edition" of his quarterly newsletter free (usually five dollars) to readers of *Hunting the Headhunters*. (For more on Cole, see Appendix D.)

RETAINER FIRMS: THE GENERALISTS

The following retainer firms make placements in a variety of industries. Although the largest ones cover just about every industry or function, the smaller firms may confine themselves to a handful. As always, make sure that your area of interest coincides with theirs.

Battalia & Associates
Contact Person: O. William
Battalia
275 Madison Avenue
New York, NY 10016
212-683-9440

Note: Also offices in Atlanta; Boston; Chicago; Cleveland; Dallas; Ft. Lauderdale, FL; Houston; Los Angeles; Menlo Park, CA; Morristown, NJ; Pittsburgh; San Francisco; Stamford, CT; Washington, DC; and abroad.

Bowden & Co., Inc.
Contact Person:
Otis Bowden II
5000 Rockside Road
#120
Cleveland, OH 44131
216-447-1800

Canny, Bowen, Inc.
Contact Person: Patricia
McCauley
425 Park Avenue
New York, NY 10022
212-758-3400
Note: Another office in Boston.

Boyden International
Contact Person: Putney
Westerfield
260 Madison Avenue
New York, NY 10016
212-685-3400

Christenson & Montgomery
Contact Person: Robert M.
Montgomery
466 Southern Boulevard
Chatham, NJ 07928
201-526-5545

Thorndike Deland Associates
Contact Person: Howard
Bratches
1440 Broadway
New York, NY 10018
212-840-8100

Robert W. Dingman Company,
Inc.
Contact Person:
R. W. Dingman
32131 W. Lindero
Canyon Road
West Lake Village, CA 91361
818-991-5950

Fleming Associates
Contact Person: Dick Fleming
1428 Franklin Street
Columbus, IN 47201
812-376-9061
Note: Also offices in Atlanta;
Des Moines, IA; Austin, Texas;
Louisville, KY; Metairie, LA;
Sarasota, FL; Stamford, CT.

Gilbert Tweed Associates
Contact Person: Janet Tweed
630 Third Avenue
New York, NY 10017
212-697-4260
Note: Also offices in Boston;
Winterport, ME; and
Washington, DC.

Garofolo Curtiss & Co.
Contact Person: Frank Garofolo
326 W. Lancaster Avenue
Ardmore, PA 19003
215-896-5080
Note: Also offices in Boston;
Camp Hill, PA; Naperville, IL;
Nashville, TN; Ponte Vedra
Beach, FL; Washington, DC.

Goodrich & Sherwood
Contact Person: Saul Samet
521 Fifth Avenue
New York, NY 10017
212-697-4131

Gould & McCoy
Contact Person: William Gould
551 Madison Avenue
New York, NY 10022
212-688-8671

Haley Associates
Contact Person: George Haley
375 Park Avenue
New York, NY 10152
212-421-7860

Handy Associates
Contact Person: Gerald
Simmons
245 Park Avenue
New York, NY 10167
212-867-8444

Haskell & Stern
Contact Person: Allan D. R.
Stern
529 Fifth Avenue
New York, NY 10017
212-687-7292

The Heidrick Partners, Inc.
Contact Person: Robert L.
Heidrick
20 North Wacker Drive
#4000
Chicago, IL 60606
312-845-9700

Heidrick & Struggles, Inc.
Contact Person: David R. Peasback
245 Park Avenue
New York, NY 10167
212-867-9876
Note: Also offices in Atlanta; Boston; Chicago; Cleveland; Dallas; Greenwich, CT; Houston; Los Angeles; Menlo Park, CA; San Francisco and Washington, DC.

Hodge-Cronin & Associates
Contact Person: Richard J. Cronin
6250 North River Road
Rosemont, IL 60018
312-692-2041

Ward Howell International
Contact Person: Max Ulrich
99 Park Avenue
New York, NY 10016
212-697-3730
Note: Also offices in Chicago; Dallas; Greenwich, CT; Houston; Los Angeles; San Francisco; and abroad.

Johnson Smith & Knisely, Inc.
Contact Person: Sheri Pearlman
475 Fifth Avenue
New York, NY 10017
212-686-9760

A. T. Kearney, Inc.
Contact Person: James R. Arnold
222 S. Riverside Plaza #2500
Chicago, IL 60606
312-648-0111

Note: Also offices in Atlanta; Denver; Los Angeles; Miami; New York; and Scottsdale, AZ.

Korn/Ferry International
Contact Person: Howard S. Freedman
237 Park Avenue
New York, NY 10017
212-687-1834
Note:Also offices in Los Angeles; Atlanta; Boston; Chicago; Cleveland; Dallas; Denver; Houston; Minneapolis; Newport Beach, CA; Palo Alto, CA; San Francisco; Seattle; Stamford, CT; Washington, DC; and abroad.

Lamalie Associates, Inc.
Contact Person: William G. Long
101 Park Avenue
New York, NY 10178
212-953-7900
Note: Also offices in Atlanta; Chicago; Cleveland; Dallas; and Tampa, FL.

R. H. Larsen & Associates
Contact Person: Robert H. Larsen
1040 Bayview Drive #330
Ft. Lauderdale, FL 33304
305-561-8102

Nordeman Grimm, Inc.
Contact Person: Peter Grimm
717 Fifth Avenue
New York, NY 10022
212-758-2300
Note: Another office in Chicago.

The Ogdon Partnership
Contact Person: Thomas H.
Ogdon
375 Park Avenue
New York, NY 10152
212-308-1600

Peat Marwick Main & Co.
Contact Person: Donald F.
Dvorak
303 E. Wacker Drive
Chicago, IL 60601
312-938-1000
Note: Also offices in Atlanta;
Boston; Dallas; Denver;
Hartford; Houston; Los
Angeles; Miami; Minneapolis;
Newport Beach, CA; New
York; San Francisco; and
Stamford, CT.

Paul R. Ray & Company, Inc.
Contact Person: Paul R. Ray
301 Commerce Street
#2300
Ft. Worth, TX 76102
817-334-0500
Note: Also offices in Atlanta;
Chicago; Dallas; Houston; New
York; and Los Angeles.

Russell Reynolds Associates
Contact Person: Richard S.
Lannamann
200 Park Avenue
23rd Floor
New York, NY 10166
212-351-2000
Note: Also offices in Boston;
Chicago; Dallas; Los Angeles;
Stamford, CT; Cleveland;

Washington, DC; Houston;
Minneapolis; San Francisco;
and abroad.

Sydney Reynolds Associates
Inc.
Contact Person: Sydney
Reynolds
212-697-8682
342 Madison Avenue
Suite 2001
New York, NY 10173

Ropes Associates, Inc.
Contact Person: John Ropes
333 North New River Drive East
Suite 4000
Ft. Lauderdale, FL 33301
305-525-6600

Susan Shultz & Associates
Contact Person: Susan Shultz
6001 East Cactus Wren Road
Paradise Valley, AZ 85253
602-998-1744

Paul Stafford Associates
Contact Person: Robert Flanagan
45 Rockefeller Plaza
New York, NY 10111
212-765-7700
Note: Also offices in Atlanta;
Chicago; Princeton, NJ; San
Francisco; and Washington, DC.

Spencer Stuart & Associates
Contact Person: Thomas Neff
55 East 52nd Street
New York, NY 10055
212-407-0200
Note: Also offices in Atlanta;
Chicago; Dallas; Houston; Los
Angeles; Philadelphia; San
Francisco; and Stamford, CT.

Sheila Wolf Associates
Contact Person: Sheila Wolf
300 East 75th Street
#23A
New York, NY 10021
212-517-7398

Egon Zehnder International, Inc.
55 East 59th Street
New York, NY 10022
212-838-9199
Note: International firm
headquartered in Switzerland;
other U.S. offices in Atlanta; Los
Angeles; and Chicago.

SPECIALTY FIRMS

The following firms specialize in a particular industry or function. Some work exclusively by retainer; others do both contingency and retainer searches.

AD AGENCY/MEDIA/PR

Bornholdt Shivas & Friends
Contact Person: John Bornholdt
295 Madison Avenue
#1206
New York, NY 10017
212-557-5252

Simon Rink Pajor Associates
Contact Person: Lynn Paul Simon
265 College Street
New Haven, CT 06509
203-777-3317

Jerry Fields Associates
Contact Person: Jerry Fields
515 Madison Avenue
New York, NY 10022
212-319-7600

Plaza, Inc.
Contact Person: Ellen Kirk
55 East Monroe
#3834
Chicago, IL 60603
312-263-0944

ADMINISTRATION

Joe C. Malone Associates
Contact Person: Joe Malone
1941 Bishop Lane
Louisville, KY 40218
502-456-2380

McCallie Associates, Inc.
Contact Person: Bob McCallie
11533–35 South 36th Street
Omaha, NE 68123
402-292-5050

W.F.H., Inc.
Contact Person: William
Hackbarth
800 Westhill Blvd
Appleton, WI 54915
414-731-8625

APPAREL/TEXTILE

Colton, Bernard Inc.
Contact Person: Roy C. Colton
417 Spruce Street
San Francisco, CA 94118
415-386-7400

Robert Howe & Associates
Contact Person: Robert W.
Hamill
2971 Flowers Road South
#128
Atlanta, GA 30341
404-455-6618

Jaral Fashion Personnel
Consultants
Contact Person: Joseph Morgan
443 Springfield Avenue
Summit, NJ 07901
201-273-1110

ARCHITECTURE/DESIGN

Connection Contingency Search
Contact Person: Ron Booth
5101 Jonar Court
Louisville, KY 40291
502-491-3195

Corporate Builders
Contact Person: Bill Meysing
92 S.W. Washington St.
Portland, OR 97251
503-223-4344

Design Executive Search
Contact Person: Rita Sue Siegel
60 West 55th Street
New York, NY 10019
212-586-4750

ASSOCIATION MANAGE-MENT/NONPROFIT

Development Search Specialists
Contact Person: Fred J.
Lauerman
W1072 First National Bank
Building
St. Paul, MN 55101
612-224-3750

Ketchum, Inc.
Contact Person: Calvin H.
Douglas
1030 Fifth Avenue
Pittsburgh, PA 15219
412-281-1481

Robison & McAuley
Contact Person: John H.
Robison
3100 NCNB Plaza
Charlotte, NC 28280
704-376-0059

BANKING/FINANCIAL SERVICES

Network Affiliates
Contact Person: Michael R.
Wagner
3500 North Causeway
#160
Metairie, LA 70002
504-837-8712

TBR Group, Ltd.
The Bankers Register
Contact Person: Howard Stevens
500 Fifth Avenue
New York, NY 10110
212-840-0800

Watkins & Associates
Contact Person: Michael Watkins
7322 Southwest Freeway
#620
Houston, TX 77074
713-777-5261

BROKERAGE/SECURITIES

Corporate Search Inc.
Contact Person: Don Fouracre
P.O. Box 12136
#12
Birmingham, MI 48009
313-644-7730

Rust & Associates, Inc.
Contact Person: John R. Rust
P.O. Box 9101
Libertyville, IL 60048
312-663-7373

Cadillac Associates/Search
Specialists
Contact Person: Dwight Hanna
3450 Wilshire Blvd.
#309
Los Angeles, CA 90010
213-385-9111

CHEMICAL

Fred Anthony Associates
Contact Person: Fred Anthony
P.O. Box 372
Lake Geneva, WI 53147
414-248-8133

Larson Associates
Contact Person: Ray Larson
P.O. Box 9005
Brea, CA 92621
714-529-4121

Merlin International
Contact Person: Henry Keller
185 Arch Street
Ramsey, NJ 07446
201-825-7220

COMPUTER-ASSISTED DESIGN & MANUFAC-TURING (CAD/CAM)/ ROBOTICS

Michael-Kent & Associates
Contact Person: Michael
Charnota
1409 East Capital Drive
Shorewood, WI 53211
414-962-2000

Liggett Associates
Contact Person: Mary Ann
Liggett
101 Executive Boulevard
Elmsford, NY 10523
914-347-5590

COMPUTER INDUSTRY/ EDP

EDP Consultants, Inc.
Contact Person: Ron Anderson
350 North Sunnyslope Road
#350
Brookfield, WI 53005
414-797-8855

Innovative Resources
Corporation
Contact Person: Joseph Greco
Statler Office Tower
Cleveland, OH 44115
216-621-4220

Systems One, Ltd.
Contact Person: John Dahl
2720 Des Plaines Avenue
Des Plaines, IL 60018
312-297-3626

DIRECT MARKETING

Ridenour & Associates
Contact Person: Suzanne
Ridenour
400 East Randolph St.
Suite 6B
Chicago, IL 60601
312-565-1150

Van Reypen Enterprises, Ltd.
Contact Person: Robert D.
Van Reypen
3100 Monroe Avenue
Rochester, NY 14618
716-586-8014

ENGINEERING

Aim Executive, Inc.
Contact Person: Jeff DePerro
6605 West Central Avenue
Toledo, OH 43617
419-841-5040

Search Enterprises, Inc.
Contact Person: Frank Polacek
520 Quail Ridge Drive
Westmont, IL 60559
312-573-1022

Sharrow & Associates
Contact Person: Douglas
Sharrow
24735 Van Dyke
Centerline, MI 48015
313-759-6910

FINANCE/ACCOUNTING

Joy Reed Belt & Associates
Contact Person: Joy Reed
Belt, Ph.D.
P.O. Box 18446
Oklahoma City, OK 73154
405-525-5230

Upper Midwest, Inc.
Contact Person:
Floyd Robertson
12 South Sixth Street
#626
Minneapolis, MN 55402
612-338-6748

FOOD/BEVERAGE

Image Support Systems
Contact Person: Wallace A. Smith
1929 Cable Street
San Diego, CA 92107
619-226-1146

J. Lee & Associates
Contact Person: Judy Lee
P.O. Box 28334
Atlanta, GA 30358
404-237-5628

Unique, Specialty Group, Inc.
Contact Person: Jennifer B. Flora
8765 Guion Road
Suite A
Indianapolis, IN 46268
317-875-8281

FOREST PRODUCTS/ PULP/PAPER

Headhunters National, Inc.
Contact Person: Beverly Bachand
5319 SW Westgate Drive
Portland, OR 97221
503-297-1451

HEALTH INDUSTRY

Hospital Staffing Services, Inc.
Contact Person: Jay Gershberg
24455 East Sunrise Boulevard #706
Ft. Lauderdale, FL 33304
305-564-4905

Jonas & Associates
Contact Person: Glenn Jonas
3333 North Mayfair Road
Milwaukee, WI 53222
414-257-3620

Joslin & Associates, Ltd.
Contact Person: Robert S. Joslin, Ph.D.
291 Deer Trail Court
Suite C
Barrington, IL 60010
312-382-7778

Witt Associates, Inc.
Contact Person: John Witt
724 Enterprise Drive
Oak Brook, IL 60521
312-574-5070
Note: Another office in Dallas.

HIGH TECHNOLOGY

N. Dean Davic Associates
Contact Person: Nicholas D. Davic
400 Penn Center Boulevard
Pittsburgh, PA 15235
412-824-8100

The Leslie Corporation
Contact Person: John Leslie
400 East North Belt #701
Houston, TX 77060
713-591-0915

Storti Associates
Contact Person: Michael Storti
4060 Post Road
Warwick, RI 02886
401-885-3100

Consolidated Precision
Contact Person: Al Warmington
11887 County Line Road
Gates Mills, OH 44040
216-423-1017

INSURANCE

Brytal Limited
Contact Person: Thom A. Williams
901 North Spoede Road
Suite 1001
St. Louis, MO 63146
314-569-1415

Errol Houk Associates
Contact Person: April Houk
3280 Mallard Cove Lane
Ft. Wayne, IN 46804
219-432-7666

Julian-Soper & Associates, Ltd.
Contact Person: Gracemarie
Soper
The Ice House
200 Applebee
Barrington, IL 60010
312-382-6067

LEGAL

Howard C. Bloom Company
Contact Person: Howard Bloom
12201 Merit Drive
#240
Dallas, TX 75251
214-385-6455

InterQuest
Contact Person: Paul Kilman
270 Farmington Ave.
#305
Farmington, CT 06032
203-674-1500

Kanarek & Shaw
Contact Person: Carol M.
Kanarek
301 East 53rd Street
New York, NY 10022
212-371-0967

Thai, Inc.
Contact Person: Dale Parsons
133 East Cook Avenue
Libertyville, IL 60048
312-680-7177

MANUFACTURING/ OPERATIONS

The Borton Wallace Company
Contact Person: Murray B. Parker
22 Broad Street
Asheville, NC 28801
704-252-5831

Stevens & Associates
Contact Person: C. H. Stevens
1016 South Eighth Street
Rogers, AR 72756
501-636-4700

W. J. Vogeler & Associates
Contact Person: Walt Vogeler
P. O. Box 37671
Omaha, NE 68137
402-895-1091

MANAGEMENT INFORMATION SYSTEMS

Bay Search Group
Contact Person: Ford K. Sayre
112 Union Street
#501
Providence, RI 02903
401-751-2870

John J. Davis Associates
Contact Person: John J. Davis
200 Park Avenue
#303E
New York, NY 10166
212-286-9489

PACKAGING

Grantham & Company, Inc.
Contact Person: John D.
Grantham
27 Eastowne Drive
Chapel Hill, NC 27514
919-489-1991

Recruiters International Inc.
Contact Person: Ron Loehr
1428 US 33 North
Benton Harbor, MI 49022
616-927-3106

PERSONNEL/HUMAN RESOURCES

J. R. Brody & Associates
Contact Person: James R. Brody
443 Springfield Avenue
Summit, NJ 07901
201-522-0450

Romeo-Hudgins & Associates, Inc.
Contact Person: Paul C. Romeo
900 East Eighth Avenue
#300
King of Prussia, PA 19406
215-337-1560

Charles Russ Associates, Inc.
Contact Person: Charles F. Russ, Jr.
1820 W. 91st Place
Kansas City, MO 64114
816-523-4001

PURCHASING/ MATERIALS MANAGEMENT

Line Management Company
Contact Person: Anthony Scott
1880 Century Park East
#212
Los Angeles, CA 90067
213-552-2009

Whitlow & Associates
Contact Person: H. T. Whitlow
3390 Peachtree Road NE
#236
Atlanta, GA 30326
404-262-2566

R&D

The Executive Search Group
Contact Person: E. R. Bower
P. O. Box 59927
Dallas, TX 75229
214-353-9330

Jim King & Associates
Contact Person: Jim King
1840 Gulf Life Tower
Jacksonville, FL 32207
904-398-7371

REAL ESTATE

Continental Search Associates, Inc.
Contact Person: William Dewey
P.O. Box 413
Birmingham, MI 48012
313-644-4506

Ken Richardson, Inc.
Contact Person: Kenneth E. Richardson
7501 Democracy Blvd.
#116
Bethesda, MD 20817
301-365-2116

Huey Enterprises
Contact Person: Arthur Huey
273 Clarkson Executive Park
Ellisville, MO 63011
314-394-9393

RETAIL/HOSPITALITY

Michael Kosmetos & Associates
Contact Person: Michael
Kosmetos
333 Babbitt Road
Suite 3001
Cleveland, OH 44123–1682
216-261-1950

SALES & MARKETING

Management Resource Planners
Contact Person: Steven A. Jablo
14755 Preston Road
#455
Dallas, TX 75240
214-239-3591

National Recruiters, Inc.
Contact Person: Tim Richards
400 Interchange South
#325
Minneapolis, MN 55426
612-546-2541

Sales Executives, Inc.
Contact Person: Dale E. Statson
755 West Big Beaver Road
2107
Troy, MI 48084
313-362-1900

Joel Wilensky Associates
Contact Person: Joel H. Wilensky
P.O. Box 155
Sudbury, MA 01776
617-443-5176

TELECOMMUNICATIONS

Richard Farber Associates
Contact Person: Richard J. Farber
60 Cutter Mill Road
Great Neck, NY 11021
516-466-3690

First Search, Inc.
Contact Person: Al Katz
4200 West Peterson
#100
Chicago, IL 60646
312-282-8810

Xagas & Associates
Contact Person: Steve Xagas
701 East State Street
Geneva, IL 60134
312-232-7044

APPENDIX A:
FOR HELP IN SELECTING A SEARCH FIRM

1. Talk to people in your professional organizations and trade association. Are there any recruiters they can recommend or call on your behalf? Are there any they advise you to be wary of? Are any recruiters members of one of the professional or-

ganizations to which you also belong? Some association news-
letters will occasionally run job listings from recruiters. Find
out if yours is one that does.

2. Talk to colleagues who have hired recruiters to fill positions. They're likely to have interviewed a number of recruiters and will be able to tell you their impressions of a
range of people in your area. A call from a client to a recruiter
on your behalf will almost certainly result in a courtesy interview.

3. Talk to friends who have worked with recruiters—both successfully and not so successfully. What were their experiences? Who was receptive? Who was not?

4. Read the advertisements in professional or trade journals.
(*The Institutional Investor* often runs ads of firms in the financial area, for instance. In the legal area, *The National Law
Journal* and *The American Lawyer* run yearly issues devoted
to search firms.) But don't rely on the ads alone. Do you know
anyone who has had dealings with these firms?

5. Keep an annotated file of names and numbers of recruiters
who have called you or whose names you come across in the
ways listed above.

6. If you are working with an outplacement firm, ask if the
counselors there have developed a list of search firms they
have found to be particularly receptive to people in outplacement.

7. After you've done the above and narrowed down your list,
call the search firms to ask the questions listed in Appendix B.

8. Consult the resources listed in Appendix D.

APPENDIX B:
QUESTIONS TO ASK BEFORE WRITING A
SEARCH FIRM

1. Verify the firm's name, address, and telephone number. If
someone has given you a recruiter's name, confirm that he is
still there. Recruiters move on in their careers, too.

2. Make sure that the firm conducts searches in your particular area of expertise. Why waste everyone's time by writing to a company that specializes in manufacturing when your field is marketing? Similarly, check that the firm handles searches in your geographical area or in the city to which you wish to move. If you're seeking a position in Chicago, but the firm concentrates on Los Angeles, you may be wasting your time.

3. Get the name of the *specific* person at the firm who specializes in your area of expertise. This is particularly important at large firms that employ many recruiters, each of whom may concentrate on different industries or functions.

4. Ask about the firm itself. How long has it been in business? What kinds of jobs, salary levels, and levels of responsibility are handled?

5. Ask for a company brochure. It will often include the firm's history, its specialty fields, and the names of the main recruiters.

APPENDIX C: QUESTIONS TO ASK WHEN A RECRUITER CALLS

1. Are you a retainer or a contingency firm?

2. Are you calling about a specific position?

3. Can you tell me a bit more about your firm? In what areas do you specialize? How long have you been in business?

4. Can you tell me a bit more about the position in question? Level of responsibility? Salary range? Why is this position open? How long has it been open? How long has it been out to search?

5. Are you calling me as a potential candidate or as a source?

6. Could you send me a description of the job so I can think about it?

7. Before we hang up, I want to make sure I have your name and firm spelled correctly. Could you give that to me again? And let me check your telephone number, too, while we're at it.

APPENDIX D:
FOR FURTHER INFORMATION ON
RECRUITERS

James Kennedy's annually updated directory of executive recruiters, which contains the names of about two thousand firms, is considered a standard reference in the industry. Insiders refer to it as "the red book." Kennedy also publishes *Executive Recruiter News*, a widely read (and sometimes controversial) industry newsletter. Its target audience is recruiters, not job seekers, but it will give anyone interested in the field an insider's view of the industry. In addition to his *Directory*, each year Kennedy selects a list of what he considers to be the country's leading fifty search firms.

Kennedy & Kennedy
Consultants News
Templeton Road
Fitzwilliam, New Hampshire 03447
Telephone: (603) 585-2200.

Kenneth J. Cole publishes a variety of directories useful to the job seeker. Instead of a single all-inclusive volume, he offers a series of about sixty separate lists of recruiting firms, focusing on specific industries, functions, specialty areas, or types of firms. They are updated approximately three times a year. Another publication, *Independent Researchers and Services*, provides a listing of independent researchers. He also publishes a quarterly newsletter, *The Recruiting and Search Report*. (For more on Cole, see Chapter 7.)

Kenneth J. Cole
The Recruiting and Search Report
P.O. Box 9433
Panama City Beach, Florida 32407
Telephone: (904) 235-3733

For those who own a computer, there is *The Executive Search System*, a data base program that contains information about approximately fifteen hundred executive-search firms. The program allows you to target a subset of search firms based on industry specialty, position or functional specialty, minimum salary of positions handled, geographical location, whether the firm is retainer or contingency, and so on. You can then print envelopes, mailing labels, and cover letters based on information from the program. The data base is updated every two months and costs $75.

Executive Search System
Custom Databanks, Inc.
127 East 59th Street
New York, New York 10022
Telephone: (212) 888-1650

The Fordyce Newsletter, published by Paul Hawkinson, addresses itself to professionals across the entire spectrum of personnel, search, recruiting, and outplacement fields. He tracks the full range of employment agencies—some 26,000 of them, "from Bob's Jobs to Korn/Ferry," as he puts it—in his quarterly *Employment Marketplace*.

The Fordyce Newsletter
P.O. Box 31011
St. Louis, Missouri 63131
Telephone: (314) 436-4044

The Headhunters by John A. Byrne (Macmillan, 1986) gives a critical overview of the industry as a whole and the giant firms in particular. Other helpful books about executive search include *Stalking the Headhunter* by John Tarrant (Bantam), *The Headhunter Strategy* by Kenneth J. Cole (Wiley), and *How to Get a Headhunter to Call* (Wiley) by Howard S. Freedman, a partner at Korn/Ferry.

Several associations may also provide helpful information, including membership directories and copies of their code of ethics:

The Association of Executive Search Consultants, founded in 1959, is the best-known professional group in the industry. About sixty retainer-search firms belong. The Association's membership directory includes a code of ethics and professional practice guidelines.

The Association of Executive Search Consultants
Janet Jones-Parker, Executive Director
17 Sherwood Place
Greenwich, Connecticut 06830
Telephone: (203) 661-6606

The National Association of Executive Recruiters, with approximately one hundred member firms, contains both retainer and contingency firms.

The National Association of Executive Recruiters
John Dugan, Chairman
J. H. Dugan Associates
505 N. Lakeshore Drive
Chicago, Illinois 60611
Telephone: (312) 222-1566

The National Association of Corporate and Professional Recruiters includes as members senior-level human-resource executives and executive-search consultants.

National Association of Corporate
and Professional Recruiters
Linda J. Meagher, executive director
146 Blackberry Drive
Stamford, Connecticut 06903
Telephone: (203) 329-2349

The National Association of Personnel Consultants publishes a *Career Guide Handbook*, which includes a membership list divided by specialty. This list does not distinguish between executive search firms and employment agencies, however, except for a short listing of retainer firms.

National Association of Personnel Consultants
Roundhouse Square
1432 Duke Street
Alexandria, Virginia 22314
Telephone: (703) 684-0180

For more information on independent researchers, you might also want to contact the Research Roundtable, a group of New York-area researchers in the executive-search industry. The Roundtable publishes a directory listing about twenty independent researchers.

The Research Roundtable
P.O. Box 3565 Grand Central Station
New York, New York 10163